Resilient
WOMEN
In Life & Business

18 Successful Business Women
Share Their Best Thinking And Strategies
To Build An Inspiring Life And Business

WM

Resilient Women In Life And Business

First published in March 2023

WM Publishing

ISBN 978-1-914265-51-8 Pbk
ISBN 978-1-914265-50-1 eBk

Editors: Kim Hayden, Cari Frame and Andrew Priestley

The rights of Jen Buck CMT CPC, Amy Siewe, Baljit Joshi, Cari Frame, Diana L Howles, Estela Dalayoan-Pinlac, Lisa Marie Gilbert, Shenneile Henry, Whitney Elkins-Hutten Ph.D, MPH, Kylie Denton, Christine Cowern, Sheron Kenny, Alessandra Wall Ph.D, Katt Phillipps, Sammy Blindell, Elena Meskhi, Susan Routledge and Kim Hayden to be identified as contributing authors of this work have been asserted in accordance with Sections 77 and 78 of the Copyright Designs and Patents Act, 1988.

A CIP catalogue record for this book is available from the British Library.

Contents

Foreword

Jen Buck CMT, CPC

I always thought I was resilient... until I wasn't.

I grew up with seven boys in my close-knit, extended family and I was at the bottom of the heap. I could run as fast, hit as hard, and hang in there when they got rowdy. I was mouthy and tough, never giving in or backing down, and always seen as an equal. I built a strong sense of self, and a strong comfort with fear, very early on in life. I always felt like a little warrior and it was fully celebrated in my family.

When I got to grade school, I was told that I was too much, too loud, too aggressive, too hard-headed, and too much like the boys. I was sent home from kindergarten with a note pinned to my shirt that encouraged my mom to 'break my spirit' which we still laugh about to this day. I eventually became softer; not because I was forced to by my family, but because I understood the pressure to fit in and get along.

5

As I grew older the messages got more confusing, and sadly, louder. I understood from society that I wasn't thin enough, smart enough, strong enough, or pretty enough. I even remember my high school counselor telling me to choose something that didn't require a college degree. Ultimately, the message I received was that I wasn't enough.

The mixed messages for women and girls are confusing, even before we hit the workplace. As we enter the corporate world we see all the signs pointing to traditional roles where men are in positions of power, strategic maneuvering is the norm, and the corporate culture seems to exclude women from most spaces of influence and proximity to the highest levels of leadership. While I am very optimistic about women in the workplace, I still know that it takes resilience to figure out the rules, strategies to move the needle forward, and allies to support us within this highly complicated space.

I had a lucky break early on in my career. At 18 years old, while attending college, I was given the opportunity to work for a start-up. I was put on a team of twenty women and they were the highest performing team in the organization, receiving award after award, every year. I learned from these women how to navigate, pivot, maneuver, and ultimately win in business. Resilience was the name of the game in the chaotic and constantly changing start-up world, and the intersection of that valuable and necessary skill was amplified as I was part of an all-female team.

I learned during those ten years that our lives will shrink or expand in direct proportion to our ability to be resilient. Our ability to trust that we have a wellspring of courage and bravery within us to tackle anything, is exactly what builds resilience. Learning to bounce back and try again when failure strikes, being willing to step into uncertainty, and finding the stimulation and excitement in situations that induce fear, is where we have to get comfortable.

Never before have we seen so many opportunities for women to lead in business and yet women still tend to be more risk-averse and prone to stepping away from instability, insecurity, or lack of certainty, much more so than their male counterparts. More than ever, we need women to be willing to lean bravely into the unknown.

I want you to step all the way in as you are reading through this book, *Resilient Women In Life And Business*. The goal that these authors have for you is to encourage you to see, feel and experience your power—and ultimately help you build your resilience—so that you can achieve all that you're aspiring to in your career. Most of us were taught to avoid potential failure at all cost, so I realize how difficult this is. However, with practice, we see the opportunity to expand our boundaries tremendously by trusting ourselves and stepping into the unknown with courage and optimism. It can feel like jumping into the deep end without our floaties or climbing a mountain without a trail map. The difference is when we are fully prepared, and willing to be uncomfortable, we have the ability to achieve more than we ever thought possible... that's when our lives start to change.

So, let's talk about what holds us back. Very simply: fear.

If we're honest, scary things invoke super-charged emotions that make us feel unstable. Sometimes fear is necessary and valid, like when we're walking alone at night and get that heebie-jeebie alarm that tells us to be on high alert. Ultimately, fear benefits us in those instances. Because we live in a culture that thrives on fear-mongering, some people find themselves feeling and acting as if every decision could cause a catastrophe. This habit of 'catastrophizing' often leads us to become afraid of any opportunity that we can't control or guarantee. While this extreme response to instability may not fully resonate with you, we still need to be able to reframe fear and find ways to get stimulated by the experience, instead of being paralyzed by it. If we break it down, fear is just another emotion and feeling. The more we step into uncertain and scary situations, the more we will build our resilience to that emotion and feeling. Resilience is the outcome of building our comfort with fear and instability.

I remember a time in my thirties when I lost my resilience. I had suffered a major loss in my life and I came to a place where my self-esteem and self-worth had become nonexistent. I was feeling a tremendous sense of failure and fear about the future, which was paralyzing. I decided to do something radical and I moved out of state, to a city I had never lived in, and committed to making the next year all about regaining my courage and building my resilience. I had spent my life surrounded by throngs of people and my ability to find confidence in being alone in my own skin was missing. I was being driven by fear and I knew this wasn't my natural state of being. So, that year was dedicated to building my resilience muscles back up by consistently putting myself in uncomfortable situations. I went to movies, dinners, concerts, and events alone. I started painting and drawing, which I hadn't done since I was young. I started cold-calling companies and individuals on my 'Dream Clients' list and asking for meetings, with a shaking voice. I even took surfing lessons because sharks were my greatest fear in life! I was doing everything I could to exercise my bravery, knowing that the outcome would be increased resilience.

I recall the last day of my surfing lessons like it was yesterday. I had never really gotten good at the sport, but I was enjoying the water without fear, which was the ultimate goal. It was time for my final ride. As I was paddling in on my belly to catch the last wave, I took one last look over my right shoulder and was prepared to pop up and plant my feet on the board, when my worst fear happened. Right at that moment, looking back into the wave, the biggest, scariest, grayest, Jen-eating fish came jumping out of that wave, landing just feet from my board. I froze, legs and arms pulled in. I had a ringing in my ears that was piercing.

My body was shaking uncontrollably and I convinced myself that I had always known this would be the death of me. I was experiencing physical paralysis and everything was just out of focus. At some point my surf instructor was at my board yelling, 'Jen! You got the gift! The universe gave you the gift! It was a dolphin, Jen! Your job here is done!'

I got the gift.

That exact moment is the defining line between lost and found, for me. That's the moment that brought me back to understanding who I was put on this planet to be. I had lost my way, but twelve months of intention and constant willingness to be uncomfortable, culminated within the gift of that big, beautiful, gray dolphin that landed next to me. Remember, resilience is the outcome of building our comfort with fear and instability. I did it. I got it.

So, let's get you closer to your gift. It begins by getting clear about what we most want in life and then identifying fears and obstacles that may be holding us back from having it. The clearer we are about what is holding us back, the more effective we'll be in moving forward.

Following, you'll find my daily tips to build resilience and find your power:

Build Your Proficiency

To build proficiency, we have to develop a set of skills to help us trust our judgments and make responsible choices. Which skills can you improve upon to feel a stronger sense of competence? This is where we have to be very honest with ourselves.

Build Your Confidence

We gain confidence by demonstrating proficiency in real-life situations. Are you confident in your skills? Do you need to up your game to feel more impressive? Do others see you as a leader or expert? How can you showcase your abilities?

Build Your Network

Connection to family, friends, and community provide a sense of security and belonging. Who can you bring in as a confidant and ally as you build your confidence and resilience? Do you have someone who can give you support and direct feedback that's rooted in love?

Build Your Broader Community

Having a sense of purpose is a powerful motivator and creates a strong sense of internal satisfaction. Contributing increases our commitment and sense of community. Are you allowing yourself to contribute to the things that matter, outside of your home and career?

Build Your Endurance

When people learn to endure fear, they are better prepared to handle adversity and setbacks. How is your ability to look on the bright side? Are you flexing your optimism muscle regularly? Are you able to get back up and brush yourself off?

Build Your Bravery

Tap into the adventurer within you. What have you always wanted to do? What's on that Bucket List? When we attempt new things, we experience excitement and stimulation. Before you know it, the feeling of fear becomes exhilarating and something you crave.

Do more of this.

Building resilience is really about stringing lots of little moments together that allow us to step outside of our comfort zone and flex our bravery and courage. As we've heard before, achieving anything worthwhile takes thousands of small brave steps and hard work. Being resilient isn't about pretending that bad things don't happen. It is, however, about being willing to lay our vulnerability on the line for something greater than our fear of failure. It's the ability to withstand hardship and get back up after we've been knocked down. The willingness to risk failure and rejection in order to achieve our greatest aspirations is at the heart of building our resilience.

Ultimately, with practice and dedication, we can all become more resilient—the more often we practice being brave, the stronger our resilience will get. The more resilient we are, the more women we can bring with us. The more women we bring, the closer we'll be to changing the world for women in business.

Onward, warrior... lean all the way in!

About Jen Buck CMT CPC

With over 30 years of experience as an award-winning Professional Speaker and Certified Master Trainer, Jen Buck began the first decade of her career in a startup where she helped launch a billion dollar global and award-winning brand while in a leadership development role. She has  since launched an online learning academy for women, founded a nonprofit, and sits on the executive board for three organizations. She's a best-selling author with six publications, has a television show that's seen in 50 countries worldwide, and is the host of a podcast that highlights female leaders who are changing their corner of the world. Along with working with some of the largest brands in the world, she has trained and coached 4- and 5-Star Generals, the highest-level executives at Coca-Cola, Mercedes, McDonalds, Walmart, Google, Yale University, and even an Emmy nominated actress—the demand for her knowledge and perspective is very broad.

Website *https://www.jenbuckspeaks.com*

SociaTap *https://sociatap.com/JENBUCK/*

Instagram: *https://instagram.com/jenbuckspeaks?utm_ medium=copy_link*

Facebook: *https://www.facebook.com/JenBuckSpeaks*

LinkedIn: *www.linkedin.com/in/jenbuckspeaks*

Clubhouse: *https://www.clubhouse.com/@ jenbuckspeaks?utm_medium=ch_profile&utm_ campaign=yWciL9L2Adnh8m-puiHASA-88985*

YouTube: *https://youtube.com/c/JenBuckSpeaks*

Online academy for women:

The HERstory Collaborative

https://www.theHERstorycollaborative.com

Podcast: The HERstory Collaborative

https://www.jenbuckspeaks.com/podcast

Leap Off YOUR Cliff
And Land In Your Best Life!

Amy Siewe

Python!!!!!!

I slam my truck into park on the dark and deserted two lane highway. It's midnight on a hot and humid south Florida night. I jump out as the tail of a python slowly slithers under the guardrail. The python makes its way towards the canal.

It doesn't know that I'm there... yet.

Holy shit this is a *big* snake. Eleven feet.

Adrenaline starts racing through me with excitement, challenge and anticipation. As I silently sneak up from behind, the python senses me. It starts to dive into the canal. I make a mad dash to grab it in the only place I could, and the worst place when given a choice... *its middle.*

This giant snake has huge teeth and a striking distance that puts me in the perfect spot to be bitten. I have no choice. If he slips into the canal he'll be gone forever.

As I grab him, he spins around and strikes at me so I can see his mouth full of razor-sharp teeth! I dodge out of the way while still holding his middle. He strikes again and I dodge the other way. He tries to make a break for the canal. I yank him back and he strikes again, missing me by a centimeter. I have to get his head under control, but right now I'm just playing defense. He hisses with every strike. Sweat is pouring down my face. After what seems like forever, he finally starts to wear out. Thank God.

With his next strike, he pauses, and I can put my foot behind his head and pin him to the ground. I am holding his middle with my right hand and grab him behind the neck with my left hand under my boot. Finally, he can't bite me, and I wrestle him into the bag. I can't help but smile as I sit on the guard rail catching my breath with the bag of snake in front of me.

Yeah, this is my happy place.

I know what you're thinking. *WTF??!!!* I was living a content and happy life as a realtor and then out of the blue, I dropped everything and took a running leap off a cliff as fast and high as I could. I was following a powerful gut feeling that my best life was over that cliff. I figured that I would either grow wings, realize it was only a few feet down, or land on a gigantic bubble house. Whatever it was, I was pretty sure I would be fine.

Let's start at the beginning.

When most six-year-old girls were playing with Barbies, I was playing with the snakes, frogs, and crawdads that my dad taught me how to catch. I had an obsessive fascination with snakes that is difficult to explain. It's like the interior designer that can instinctively put a room together, or the musician that plays a song without reading music. I was just born with this passion and fascination. I wanted to learn all I could about all kinds of snakes. I spent so much of my time in the creeks and woods in the Midwest searching for snakes, catching them, observing them, and letting them go. I worked in the exotic pet industry in college and after that, it was always a hobby that I never outgrew.

At the end of 2018, I was happy with my life. I had a successful real estate business for thirteen years in Indianapolis, with a massive client base and community influence. All of my goals and plans revolved around growing my business and team. I could do without the cold Indiana winters that seem to go on forever, but other than that, life was good.

One day I read about someone catching a python in Florida on social media. That stopped me in my tracks. Wait… *What???!! There are wild pythons in Florida???*

I found out that Burmese pythons are an invasive species in Florida. They are originally from southeast Asia and in 1992 when hurricane Andrew demolished a breeding facility, hundreds of Burmese pythons landed in the Everglades. As of now there are an estimated one hundred to three hundred thousand pythons in South Florida. They have eaten ninety eight percent of the mammals in some areas. It is a colossal problem and is destroying the precious Florida Everglades ecosystem. In response, the state started a pilot program in 2017 and hired twenty-five hunters to attempt to get a handle on the situation.

I had to see it for myself and find out more, so in January of 2019 I booked a vacation with my fiancé, Dave, in south Florida. Even though Dave isn't a snake guy, he is an outdoorsman and loves my passion. I looked up some local hunters and Donna Kalil, who was part of the state program, agreed to take us on a python hunt. That morning when she pulled up in her 1998 Ford Expedition with a custom ladder attached to the back to climb up to the giant python perch fixed to the roof, I was in awe. This was for real!

I didn't realize that hunting pythons meant standing on a truck roof going five miles per hour, looking over the sides of a one lane gravel levee that stretched endlessly into the middle of the swamp. The pythons are captured live and dispatched later, so firearms aren't used in the field. It's like no other type of hunting in the world.

It is now 5pm. We have been out there for eight hours and no pythons. Even though I felt like I was floating, I was slightly deflating. Maybe this is just a fun vacation excursion and that's the end. I'm lost in these thoughts when Donna yells, *'PYTHON!!!!'*

She slams on the brakes and nearly sends Dave and I flying over the front of the truck. She is pointing as she throws it in park, and I follow her finger to the one thing that I have been trying so hard to imagine. There it is. The unmistakable pattern of a Burmese python. It's the biggest snake I have ever seen in the wild. Nine magnificent feet of sheer power, ready to fight.

Adrenaline and instinct kicked in. I rushed down the ladder and got up close to Donna as she was already stalking it from behind. She suddenly makes her move and grabs it behind the head, so I lunge for the tail. This powerful snake is writhing and hissing and trying to break free with all its might. Its strength is mind-blowing, but we have it secured so it can't get away.

It is the most glorious moment of my life! *This is it!!! This is my calling!!! Holy Shit!* My brain is exploding! I want to jump up and down and scream to the world!!! I was on cloud nine for the whole rest of the vacation.

I absolutely knew that hunting pythons in Florida was where I belonged. It's all I could think about. This fascination I have with snakes has been a hobby for most of my life, but this is the chance for me to use my passion and actually make a difference. I would be such an asset because I'm not afraid of the gigantic constrictors, I know so much about them, and I'm obsessed with learning more and more. A few days after returning home, I told Dave that I had to move to Florida to figure out how to be a python hunter because there was nothing I could do from Indiana that would help me. He just smiled and told me he knew that we were moving to Florida the moment he saw the smile of pure joy on my face after catching that python.

Within six weeks I sold my real estate client database, rented a room from a guy in Miami that I found online, packed a few things, and drove down to Florida to start my new life. Dave couldn't join me yet, since he still had his business to run in Indiana.

Looking at this decision logically, it was ridiculous and insane. The python hunting program was a trial and no one could tell me if it was going to continue or if they would ever hire additional hunters. I didn't have a job lined up. I didn't know the area or where to hunt pythons. I didn't know anyone, including the people I was going to live with. I could have been murdered and dumped in the swamp and no one would ever know.

The thing that made all of that irrelevant is that I knew in the deepest part of my heart that this was the next chapter in my life. I had an overwhelming sense of urgency and, at the same time, I felt this incredible sense of harmony, like every puzzle piece in my life just instantly and easily fell into place. I had no idea what my life would look like or what opportunities awaited. I trusted myself to figure it out, and I did.

How do you know when it's right? *You. Just. Absolutely. Know.* Like nothing you have ever known in your life. Obstacles are easy, excuses don't exist, and fear takes a backseat.

Since moving to Florida, I have racked up more accomplishments than I can believe. I was one of the second round of twenty-five hunters hired by the state and have caught over 400 pythons, the biggest one being 17'3, 110 lbs. (by myself). I have raised $315,000 by donating hunts to charity auctions. I have been featured on many TV programs, documentaries, magazine articles and podcasts, including the Today show, Fox and Friends, CNBC, Reader's Digest and Time Magazine. Out of my love of snakes and a desire to make something good from their demise, I figured out how to use their skin to make leather products. I make the only Apple watch band in the world made from invasive python skin. I am a public speaker and a published author.

I followed my passion and I am living my absolute best life as the Python Huntress, all because I took that leap. After all, what's the worst that could happen? I would figure out how to climb back up and find another cliff.

About Amy Siewe

Amy Siewe is a professional python hunter in south Florida, hired to catch and euthanize the invasive and destructive Burmese pythons that are destroying Florida's ecosystem.

She has caught over 400 pythons, the biggest being 17'3, 110lbs (by herself), has raised $315,000 by donating hunts to charity auctions, has been featured on many TV programs, documentaries and magazines articles, including the Today show, Fox and Friends, CNBC, Reader's Digest, and Time Magazine. She is a public speaker and published author.

She has made it her mission to find a use for the pythons and has designed the only Apple watch band in the world made from the skin of the invasive pythons.

Email: *info@pythonhuntress.com*

Website: *www.pythonhuntress.com*

Facebook: *https://www.facebook.com/amy.siewe*

Instagram: *https://www.instagram.com/ thepythonhuntress/*

LinkedIn: *https://www.linkedin.com/in/amy-siewe/*
Twitter: *https://twitter.com/amysiewe*

YouTube Channel: *https://www.youtube.com/channel/ UCAO5dypbFpI6YrdPOd5zCkw*

Love, Life and Business
How I Conquer Balance
And Prosperity

Baljit Joshi

Owning your own business sounds like a dream to many, but the reality is far less dreamy. The time freedom you get from setting your own hours and not answering to anyone sounds like the perfect job. However, past the sunshine and rainbows, there is so much hard work behind the scenes on a day-to-day basis that catches many new entrepreneurs off guard, and they begin to drown as soon as they jump in.

I am a real estate agent with over half a decade of business experience and it has been a rollercoaster of highs and lows. When I first started in real estate, I was 26 years old, married without children and living out of my in-law's basement. I am a born and raised Calgarian, who graduated from the University of Calgary in Science and Fine Arts, with Marketing at SAIT. I decided to change my career direction into a space where I could utilize my diverse education and work experience in customer service and finance, to work for myself and serve others. I was grateful and thrilled to start my journey to build a business in real estate in order to empower people with the right knowledge to help achieve their next big milestone in life. Despite my excitement, my first year was a total bust. Getting into the real estate industry, there wasn't much support outside of the education taught in licensing until recently. At the time, I barely had support from my brokerage on how to build a business and make my first paycheque. I didn't even know what to do on a day-to-day basis. It wasn't until I met my first mentor who took me under her wing and showed me what the day-to-day looked like as an agent. Here, there were no allocated tasks on a daily basis. Rather, it was what the business called for and how I wanted to structure my day.

During the inception of my business, my relationship with my husband was going well; we had time to spend with one another, watch movies whenever we wanted to and enjoyed eating out at new restaurants and dreaming of our future life together. At the end of my second year as a real estate agent, we found out that I was pregnant. We built a plan to move into a home of our own before the baby was born. Keep in mind that, as a couple, we had not had true privacy during these foundational years. We were living in a house with six other people, which presented its own challenges. When I agreed to marry my husband, it was because we were going to live with his parents 'for a bit' until we figured out what we wanted to do. That 'bit' lasted four years.

It was a relief to be moving into my own space without feeling like a glass ceiling over my head. Although I was excited to finally have my own place, I was feeling totally unprepared, anxious and uncertain as to how my life was going to change when my baby was arriving within a matter of weeks. All I could think about was, what would I do about work.

At the time, I had limited choices as I underwent a C-section. We had our baby in July 2019, and I put my real estate business on hold for nine months. I jumped back into work at the start of the COVID-19 pandemic with some urgency, as we had to let go of my husband's business due to the pandemic and unknowing what it fully entailed. At the same time the pandemic was announced, our baby underwent surgery, which put pressure on us resulting in letting my husband's business go. I was completely panicked. I took on the pressure of being a sole-provider for my family, and it freaked me out because I was afraid of failing.

All I knew at that time was that something had to change.

Later that year, I met my now mentor, who showed me a different way of business and multiple ways of generating cash-flow in real estate. I needed to be better than I was, and I had to support my family. That's all I knew.

During this unsettling and anxious time, I looked for ways to accelerate my business. With the support of my husband, I signed up for a coaching program that cost me around five-figures for the year. I could remember my stomach doing somersaults as my voice hesitated to read aloud my credit card number over the phone. I knew that this program was exactly what I was looking for and was going to help position me as a go-to real estate agent in the market space. I also knew this program was going to help my marketing efforts reach more people I could help. It wasn't cheap, and we only had one source of income at that time, which was 100% commission based on my production. It was do or die. I remember taking that leap of faith and trusting myself that I would do whatever it took to make this business a success so I could give my family some piece of mind and food on the table.

As months went by, I was so consumed in the training and coaching I was a part of, that some days I had heavy mom-guilt for not showing up as a mother in our family. I felt like the roles in our family had completely flipped as I was a sole-provider. I remember I would spend most of my day on my laptop rather than my family. I would run out of the house, not knowing what was happening around me, if there were dishes to be washed or a house to maintain, I had full blinders on and focused on the people I was serving to bring home a healthy income.

Each hectic day that went by, my husband and I drifted further away from each other.

We would get into fights about the little things like spoons. Yes, spoons! I knew he had my back, but I totally disappeared. I felt he had me 100% of the time, from bringing me food to my desk to cleaning the house, taking care of our baby, and sending picture updates throughout the day. I was always racing to 'get it all done' in my business so that I could relax after. What I failed to realize was that I was on a hamster wheel, that there never is an end to the work we do as entrepreneurs.

I was tired and grumpy even before getting out of bed, I was so drained. I was emotionally exhausted by the; arguments, fights, the stress of everything on my shoulders, and to basically be everything to everyone. Each month, our fights got worse, our relationship got worse and I didn't know what to do. I remember hearing my husband yelling no matter what I did, feeling the overwhelm of my life and my relationship crumbling down, and feeling the touch of my son grabbing onto my shirt when he got scared. I had to put a pin in my business and put focus back on my family. I knew if we didn't do something, our future was going to be more difficult. We were going down a path where we wouldn't be together, which still wouldn't resolve any of the issues within ourselves. No matter who we would be with in the future, those issues would still be there regardless.

I made a decision to get help for myself and stay committed to learning about what was happening in my life and within myself. I was open-minded and real with who I was and my own wrong-doings. This started me down a path of healing within myself and my past. There was so much to learn about myself and re-learn the truths from my limiting beliefs. I thought it was always my fault during the fights, and when I saw the whole picture, it was both of us who needed to resolve our underlying issues.

The 'D' word hung over our marriage like a threat for months. It was a dark time. We went through some couples counseling to help shift our perspectives and understand each other's truths. Around the same time, we went on a long-overdue vacation. It had been three years of working at home, new house, new baby, losing a business and re-starting business all during a pandemic. We went to Jamaica for five days on a beautiful five-star resort to celebrate my birthday when calamity struck on the third day. We were ATVing through the bumpy jungle and I veered off towards a tree, flew off the ATV and broke my wrist. At first, I thought I couldn't walk and I was completely terrified. My husband, riding in an ATV behind me, watched me crash, and quickly rushed over to me and started to assess my injuries in a panic. In this pivotal moment, we realized that our lives together were bigger than just our fights. We had a son at home, and we were scared and afraid of losing each other. So much time was wasted on stressing and fighting instead of just being happy and connecting with each other and loving one another. After we got back to the resort, my husband carefully covered my cast and helped me into a warm shower. He massaged my scalp, carefully bathed and held me. We broke down and cried together; we loved each other so much and wanted to be happy again.

I am not saying anyone needs to be in a life-threatening situation to realize how much you both mean to one another, but it's important to recognize that anything can happen to anyone at any time. We are not super-humans or invincible by any means. It felt as if we took each other for granted this whole time and we realized we really wanted to unite together as a strong and loving family. There's something to be said about seeing your loved one in pain. This was our turning point.

Through this traumatic experience, I realized that not only did I not want to be a single mom, but I also did not want to continue building my business as a sole-entrepreneur, trading my time for money. There were so many great attributes of my business I hadn't yet explored, and it was the next phase of my business I wanted to focus on. Had the incident resulted in a long-term physical issue, my business would dissolve without me and I would have nothing to show for it. This new perspective in my life brought my husband, who is also an entrepreneur, into a space where we could collaborate and work together to build our legacy through power of leverage. My husband specializes in helping people build wealth in their families through educating and empowering them. Through the power of leverage, we are both able to lean on one another to reach and impact more families in a positive way. With this mission, we are able to position our clients to utilize their dollar twice when purchasing real estate. This is what we have always wanted for our family, and this is what we are advocating to others.

As we are both entrepreneurs, personal development has always been something we strive to incorporate in our day to day. I have been on a spiritual path for decades and personal development for over half a decade. It is powerful to see how we can gain understanding for ourselves and others, all while healing our wounds with a deeper sense of understanding. For me, it was knowing myself and self-acknowledgment for others around me, that had shifted in order to become a better version of myself. When I decided to strive to be the best version of myself, I started to positively affect everyone else around me. Although it's very difficult to see the sides of ourselves that are so ingrained in us that we don't acknowledge otherwise is how change is born through awareness.

Relationships are ever-changing, growing, dying, starting, ending, and essential. We have been taught love, through our parents, from the day we were born and have been thrown into a world where so many different and strong emotions are present each day. As entrepreneurs, it's part of our business to cultivate new relationships and/or partnerships on a regular basis to thrive in this unpredictable world of business. I realize through all the different types of clients I have helped in my career thus far, that each person is meeting you at a different level of their own self-awareness. I also noticed that the more self-work

I did on myself, reflected the type of client I was also attracting. Although these relationships are important, we have our friends, families, and spouses which carry a significant role in how we portray ourselves to clients and to ourselves. The most important relationship you can have, is the one with yourself, yet how many of us stop to look at ourselves in the mirror in the eye to say, *'Hi, how you doin'? No, really, how are YOU doing?'*. To care and love ourselves. The amount of love we pour into ourselves matters, how much we fill our cups is directly correlated to the energy we put out into the world.

Many of the mindset and business tools and resources I have gathered over the years have led me through a path of self-awareness, and awareness of others on a deeper level to in turn allow me to better serve the needs of my clients. The work I do on myself is all based on psychology and the mind. By understanding myself more, I am able to understand others better.

In a world of chaos, busy schedules, demands of clients and family, I am not left with very much time to give myself to reflect and breathe. I noticed that when I carve out ten to thirty minutes of space and time in the mornings or at the end of the day for myself, it gives me time to reflect and have a deeper understanding of how to align myself with my day-to-day actions and overall goals in my life. During this time, I journal for at least ten minutes to let go of whatever is on my mind, and to get it out on paper. For the remainder of the twenty minutes, I meditate to start my day with a blank slate, so it brings clarity to any decision making the day brings.

This time is the most precious and valuable time to fill my cup with positive fulfilling energy in order to conquer my day, and conquer my life.

My business evolves as I evolve, and there were some major factors that contributed to the success in making over six-figures in my last year, as a result of the work I put into myself in the course of only two years. One underlying key to keep a successful marriage and a growing business was setting a schedule to connect with my husband every other week for a date night, which meant no kids. I scheduled it in the calendar for the year for both of us to recognize and plan together.

With scheduling my work, an excellent tool to keep my busy life on track was time blocking. This strategy is powerful in time management of life and business. It allows me to have space where I need it, and flexibility where it's most essential. A key strategy I use to keep me on track with my schedule is to select three business priorities for the day, and two personal ones to schedule out the night before. One simple technique I use when my task starts, I put away any distractions and implement the Pomodoro Technique (Francesco Cirillo), which means I set a timer for twenty-five minutes to focus on that one task the entire time. When the timer goes off, I set the timer again for another five minutes to take a break. When I come back, I set it again for another twenty-five minutes and repeat the sequence for a total of four times, then take a break for an hour. In this way, I am hyper focused on getting that one task done with complete focus and attention.

Moreover, another way I maximize my time each day is by delegating tasks I don't need to do myself. I started by taking an inventory of my day of each task I've completed and rate it from one to five. Five being the highest ranking and the thing I love to do, and one being the lowest and least favorite thing I love to do. Anything that is below a three, I delegate out. An example of this is from social media marketing, cleaning the house, laundry, and client drop offs, etc. Time is the most precious commodity in the world. One of my biggest realizations was that I can maximize my time, delegate tasks to the right people, and I am in the driver seat of my life.

The last big tool is leverage. I have had the ability to leverage myself and my business to help myself and others grow to the next level. I urge you; if you have the opportunity to do this, then do it. Find key players who are game changers in the business, partner with them to grow to heights never imaginable before. Key partnerships will expand our knowledge and abilities and put us in coaching roles where we can also provide value to those who value us. The majority of wealth that is generated is leveraged through vital partnerships by providing value to those who we serve. My mission is to help more agents thrive in their business and life with a healthy balance and conquer their world. It's important to me since I was once drowning in life and wished someone could send me a safety line and guide me through the way. The Universe has blessed me with my story to touch many lives, and I believe it is up to me to pour into others along the way.

If I hadn't been able to learn these lessons over the most challenging years I faced, I wouldn't be able to level-up to the higher version of myself. I know now that as my current self, I need to be a different and better version of myself as my future self, as in someone I don't know yet. The only way to achieve this, is to push through discomfort day after day and apply the teachings from the lessons or from challenges I have in our day-to-day life. I am blessed and humbled by all the challenges in my life. as there will always be a lesson to be learned. I believe that we are dealt the cards we have because the universe believes we can handle it, and there is a lesson we need to learn to excel to the next level in our life. If I hadn't gone through these adversities, I wouldn't be the wise person I am today. I am a student of life, striving to one day become a master; that day will be my last.

About Baljit Joshi

Born and raised Calgarian, Baljit operates business as a Realtor® in Calgary and area. Seeing a need for authenticity, honesty and trust, Baljit chose to represent people with their real estate needs. As the owner of Joshi & Co, her mission is to educate her clients through a seamless process.

Her core value is to continuously grow and educate herself. This has been shown through recognition by the Calgary Herald as a Top Producing Agent. She is a Seller's Specialist, Negotiations Expert and University of Calgary Alumni in Science and Art. As a mental health advocate, she strives to bridge the gap between community and awareness. Baljit provides value and helps clients, fellow agents, and the community in any way she can. Baljit believes in giving by offering food to the homeless and families in need through her effort.

Email *baljitkjoshi@gmail.com*

Facebook *https://www.facebook.com/joshico.official*

Instagram *https://www.instagram.com/joshico.official/*

LinkedIn *https://www.linkedin.com/in/baljit-k-joshi-a2609859/*

TikTok *https://www.tiktok.com/@realtorcalgary*

Website *https://joshico.exprealty.com/*

YouTube *https://www.youtube.com/channel/UCKq0bdrdEBf1cyxSsLZULww*

The Day A River Saved Me From Drowning In Negativity

Cari Frame PCC

'You just need to love yourself more.'

So said many a kind person with the best intentions and very little understanding of what that takes. I will never forget how it felt when a personal trainer said that to me. I remember looking at her, incredulity beaming from my eyes like lasers.

I was focused on achieving my goal weight because I thought that would fix all my problems. I had been working out five days a week for months, cutting carbs, all the typical fad fixes. How am I supposed to start loving myself when all I had ever done was practice being critical, negative and only conditionally accepting of myself since I was a pre-teen? Is there a magic switch somewhere I can flick on? Is this something only rich people who pay for daily therapy can achieve?

My brain at the time, in typical unhelpful fashion, provided an answer.

It said, *Dumbass, just achieve your goal weight first, or at least get into those size 8 pants again. Then you can love yourself.* Or: *grow out that mop of frizz you call hair into some luscious golden locks and then you will achieve self-love.* But only then, not before.

To be clear, all this inner mental venom was happening behind a mask of serene positivity. To those who knew me well, I was the person to go to if you needed compassionate support, a positive outlook or connection to your own inner strengths. My wide blue eyes and welcoming smile declared warmth and belief in all good things. What they didn't know was that I could support that in others decades before I was able to do so consistently for myself. My inner negativity was like a secret snake coiled around my neck, endlessly whispering in my ear all the reasons why I was, not now and never would be, good enough.

The snake didn't debilitate me completely, except for when it did. I accomplished many excellent things between the ages of 17 to 40 but I fought an endless, exhausting inner battle every step of the way. This is the story of how I learned to not only win the battle against my own self-loathing, but help others do the same.

Have you ever watched a kid dance? A child of less than ten years of age will hear a song they like and just start grooving without a second thought. They might close their eyes, lost inside the joyful rhythm, their body moving in time. Spine, arms, legs and head, all flowing, jerking and jumping together in wild abandon.

They get caught up in the combined ecstasy of sound, beat and breath, not a single care given to how they look or how others might perceive them. They are free and it is all the sweeter because they don't even know there's anything to be free from.

Now imagine being in a store and your favourite song comes on the speakers. You can feel the music calling your body to dance, your feet or hips may even answer the call with an imperceptible shimmy. But the joy and abandon of losing yourself in the music are usually out of reach, right?

What is it that keeps you from dancing freely when a child can so easily accomplish it? What force holds you back? Are there chains on your ankles? Will you be ousted from society if seen?

It is our thoughts holding us back, of course. The airiest, lightest element imaginable, yet thoughts have the ultimate power to stop us in our tracks.

At any given moment, a thought could be percolating within you – perhaps something like this: Of course it's my own fault, I am to blame for everything wrong in my life. It's only a thought, yet it feels like a huge rock tied to your ankles, pulling you under the water.

I nearly lost myself many times from the drowning weight of my own inner haters. At 22, I was a fierce mix of optimist and old-fashioned romantic with a secret lack of self-worth.

By that time, I had cycled across central Canada, planted thousands of trees, travelled through Asia and nearly completed my degree with honours. Despite all that external progress, my inner negativity was an insidious whisper, subtle yet ever present. It encouraged me to keep my goals small, to not report the sexual assaults I had endured, and to believe my then-boyfriend when he said that his cruelty was entirely my fault.

When he said, 'If you were more caring and trustworthy, I could be nicer,' my inner critic was right there to agree with him. Be better, work harder and maybe you can be worthy of his love. When he said, 'If you complain to your family about us, you will make it impossible for us to be happy,' my inner hater said, *Right!? You deserve what's happening because YOU ARE NOT ENOUGH so don't confide in anyone.* When he would lunge for me to keep me quiet (but never hit me as that would leave evidence) my thoughts said, *Look what you made him do.*

I stayed in that abusive relationship for four years.

The 22-yr old who's heart and mind were open to all possibilities had been replaced with a 26-year-old woman that walked away from that relationship a prisoner; freed from the external cell but caged and tortured from within. Wherever I went, however much I tried to convince myself that I had made it, that I could live my own life again, the poisonous voices within were right there letting me know I didn't deserve anything good.

I ran away from the city where we'd owned a house together, taking a mapping job down south near the Waterton mountains. I knew the job had no future – I was leaving nearly all my possessions and most of my earnings behind – but I didn't feel capable of creating a future for myself anyway.

As I walked, drove and quadded the riverbanks near Cardston, accusations swirled inside my mind, a thousand tiny cuts taking their slow toll. I would ask myself over and over - *How could I be so stupid? How could I take such obvious abuse for four years, 24/7 attacks? How could I not see the pattern?* Love bombing, putting me on a pedestal, not getting everything he wanted, attacking my sense of self, making me afraid of his reactions so I'd stay compliant, then little drips of love bombing again to keep me hopeful.

Over and over, the cycle repeated, yet I stayed. In trying to be worthy of his love, I shut off all my personal relationships, some would never recover. Worst of all, I destroyed some of my travel journals because he had read a few pages and declared me a globe-trotting whore. To this day, I mourn the loss of those pages. What an idiot I had been. Around and around the negativity sucked me under like a dark and powerful current. I began to see myself as a person who could not and should not trust herself. A person who makes bad choices, who is weak and gullible. This inner turmoil was hollowing me out and I was becoming an empty shell with 'victim' stamped across my forehead.

Lying awake at night, I looked back over my life and found all the evidence any court of law would need to prove the story I was telling myself was true and accurate. I remembered every bad decision I had made (no matter how small). I recalled every time I believed in someone, and they let me down. Everywhere I looked in my past I saw failure, incurable idiocy and an alarming trend of self-destruction. I was drinking poison, one thought at a time. I shut down my inner light for good for a while. If I am a person who can't trust herself, then I can't trust anything. I could not see anything good ahead of me because I could no longer see anything good in my past.

Despite my inner exhaustion, I showed up for work every day. Mother nature was my only solace. The prairie fields hummed with subtle life as I walked mile after mile, a GPS pack on my back. The slowly flowing river current soothed my spiraling mind, while the birds kept reminding me that one's path can change, even mid-flight. I didn't stop to soak it in. I kept pushing forward without rest. The beauty was a gift I didn't feel worthy of receiving.

One midsummer day, the heat and stillness oppressive, I collapsed onto a pebbled riverbank, succumbing to my soul-deep weariness. In such a weakened state, I couldn't hold myself back from enjoying the beauty any longer. It came flooding in, the heady scents of flowers, light sparkling off the water, birds flitting by. My heart hurt from swelling so suddenly, I cried and cried. Nature had always been my church and yet in that moment I felt so unworthy where before I had always felt at home.

How did I get here? What did I do to deserve such rejection from all that is good? Inside those questions, there came a pause. A gap in the constant self-judgement where a soft, cool breeze flowed. Into that space, another, softer question came – *What made me choose him, and what made me stay?*

With a curious and hopeful heart, where judgement had no place, I began to see a truer story. I was not stupid, weak or gullible. I was (and still am) a person who believes that love means seeing the best in someone, that loyalty means staying by their side not just when it is easy. I was also a person with very little romantic experience who happened to fall in love with a very cunning, manipulative young man who wasn't capable of reciprocating healthy love.

I felt within me how true this version of the story was, my tears flowed with recognition. I was coming home to myself. I could see that I had stayed in the relationship because of how deeply I believed in him. I had been gullible, not because I was stupid, but because I was loyal and hopeful. I had been (and still was) so many good things, and it was not my fault that he twisted the good against me.

I was then able to investigate my past and see the truth of this revelation extending far back. I had lived life with an open and innocent heart. I had found good people, and I had also found bad. But through it all,

I stubbornly believed in the good in people. I believed in the power of love.

On that day, by that gentle river, I came back to myself. I was no longer a victim who was not worthy of trust. I became a survivor who trusts myself and refuses to live in fear.

I began to live this new connection to myself; a groundedness I have lived within ever since. *I am a person who cannot help but see and call out the best in people. I am a person who loves in a way that expands not just my own life but my beloved's as well. I am a woman who has had to learn some lessons the hard way.*

Imagine for a moment. If I had stayed living the story, *I am a stupid, gullible woman who can't trust herself to be anything other than a victim* – where would I be today? Take a moment to paint that picture in your mind. What would I look like? What would my life be like?

I imagine myself as having a lot more wrinkles, a lot fewer friends, very little love because I wouldn't have let it in or cultivated it. My work would be empty and unfulfilling. A very dark picture indeed.

Because of that moment on the riverbank, when I opened my heart and my mind to the kindness within, my life was forever changed.

I was able to heal from the abuse. I was able to learn to love and live with joy again. I have family and friends and work that brings me so much richness.

I support others in finding their way to self-kindness and learning to live by and act on it as often as possible.

Don't get me wrong, this is not a magic wand scenario. I did not just do this work once and feel happy and positive forever after. This work of bringing kindness, care and curiosity to ourselves is done often and has many layers. At this very moment, there are thoughts within me, prickly and barbed, trying to convince me that, *No one cares about your stupid past, just shut up and go clean your sad little single-mom house.* Writing that down actually made me laugh. What a horrendous petty thought.

Why does our own mind turn against us so easily? This is a question that has fascinated me ever since I first began to distinguish the negative from the supportive thoughts in my own head. Countless coaching clients have asked the same question in our sessions when they begin this work. It is truly bewildering that the smartest part of us can be so self-destructive. There is extensive neuroscience and psychological research that attempts to provide complex answers to this.

Let me summarize my own understanding of it.

- Our brains are systems of habit while also being ever adaptable. Neural pathways are the well-travelled, rutted roads of our brain. When you travel a self-critical path every day for years, the ruts dig deep, and your brain can steer down those paths seemingly automatically.

- The protective mechanisms in our brains that alert us to danger and keep us alive, also look for danger within us if no external danger or distraction occupies it. Since we live in a time of (relative) comfort, not to mention endless selfies, the protective brain has lots of time to find worst-case scenarios within our self-concept.

- Because these worst-case scenario thoughts are coming from within us, they feel unavoidable and true, truer, even, than a person standing in front of us complimenting us.

- When we believe the false negative thoughts we have about ourselves, we tend to act based on those negative perspectives. *Hello self-fulfilling prophecy, terrible to see you again. What? You brought your friend self-sabotage along?* Oh dear.

- Due to these negatively inspired actions, our life now corroborates the negative thoughts, making them seem even more true. We lose trust in ourselves which is a core element in confidence and the ability to make lasting positive change.

- Despite this seemingly damning cycle, our brains are also endlessly adaptable and changeable. With care and effort, the downward spiral can become a positive upward cycle.

- Shame keeps us choosing the negative, while kindness and compassion inspire positive thoughts and actions and create new neural pathways. Helping people build a practice of self-kindness is my life's work for this very reason – it changes everything!

That day so many years ago sitting by the river, I did not know any of this. I merely knew that a moment of open curiosity released me from the prison of self-judgement I had been barely surviving. A moment of grace made everything possible. A pause, a question and a wish to understand brought me back to myself.

You can do this for yourself too. Anytime. Anywhere. You don't need a river to sit by.

Just now, put your hands to your chest and press softly. Close your eyes and feel your attention settle into the warmth under your hands. Breathe and allow yourself to simply be. Not changing anything, not problem solving or being in your brain. Just being and breathing and feeling what is there. In this pause, there is connection to your deeper self. Breathe. Kindness and goodness live within you.

If this exercise served to connect you to negative thoughts, that is natural. Your goodness and light are undoubtedly in there and you just need more practice to uncover them.

This is the power of the kindness we give to ourselves. It can shape who we are, what we see as possible, and what we let in. So many things that impact our lives are not within our ability to change, but the self-kindness we live by is absolutely within our control.

As a deeply good, big-hearted woman, bringing kindness to yourself will never be selfish. It will, in fact, be the least selfish thing you can do. For when kindness helps you be more truly yourself, your whole world will benefit. The goodness will ripple out from you, inviting and inspiring kindness and bravery wherever you go.

My most profound wish for you is this: if there is a negative thought or story you have been believing that is holding you back from truly living and loving and being brave, find truer and kinder thoughts and act on those whenever you can.

About Cari Frame, PCC

Cari Frame is a professional certified coach and a published author with a life-long study of self-kindness's transformational power. The beautiful resilience born from struggle has compelled Cari's words to the page since she was in her teens and forms the foundation for her coaching programs and workshops. Everything is possible when we bring kindness to ourselves. Connect with Cari at www.cariframe.com @selfkindnesscoach

cariframe.com

https://www.facebook.com/selfkindnesscoaching

https://www.instagram.com/selfkindnesscoach/

https://www.tiktok.com/@selfkindnesscoach

https://www.linkedin.com/in/cari-frame/

Never Play the Victim

Diana L Howles

'They're not here?' I asked incredulously after arriving at the client's training site, as I began to prepare the classroom. What happened to the shipment of participant workbooks for my all-day training class? To my horror, I was informed that the boxes of workbooks, forms, and supplies had arrived the previous week, but then were mistakenly mailed back to headquarters several states away. My heart literally dropped. Those workbooks contained every handout for my training class including preparation exercises, learning activities, forms, and more. They provided the learning structure for the day and were integral to attendees' participation. Now, attendees would have nothing to reference. And that was only the beginning.

To make matters worse, for the first time ever I was walking into a training situation without the usual background knowledge. Normally, our company protocol required we reach out to clients at least two weeks before delivering a training program. We used this pre-class consult to clarify logistics, discuss the learners' needs and prior knowledge, and get a feel for their general skill level on the respective instructional topic. For this client, I had called and left voicemails, emails, and messages multiple times in the weeks and days prior but never heard back.

As a result, I felt as if I was entering this training class blindfolded. I didn't know anything about the learners, what to expect, when to meet the client on-site, how much knowledge the learners knew on the topic, or what their current challenges were. This was highly unusual, as we always customized our training approach to clients' specific needs.

Several months earlier, I was contracted to fly from my home in the northern US to southern Texas to deliver an in-person training class on presentation skills. This was a time in my professional life when I was deeply challenged by major obstacles. But it was also a time where I witnessed a powerful reversal by applying an adage that changed my life.

After arriving at the facility, I located the training room on the top floor. The room towered over downtown San Antonio, and the windows that lined the room showcased a beautiful, panoramic view of the city. I quickly scanned the room. There were approximately twenty-five young professionals clustered in small groups at the back of the room – seemingly, miles from the speaker.

Yet the chairs and tables near the front and middle of the room stood hauntingly vacant. I watched the learners' body language carefully as a speaker addressed them with opening remarks. They sat with arms folded, legs crossed, many looking down, and others multi-tasking. Their disinterest was palpable.

Unfortunately, as the opening speaker projected slides, I also noticed the data projector in the room was on the blink. Sometimes it worked, and sometimes it didn't. I would be using this same data projector for my own slide visuals. Knowing there were only minutes to go before I was introduced, my heart was pounding and the voice in my head said, *This is a disaster.*

In that moment, I knew I had a choice to make.

One option was to surrender to the situation and admit there was nothing I could do to make this training a success. After all, the client had not circled back with me on time to customize this training, the participant workbooks, supplies, and evaluations were accidentally mailed back, the data projector appeared to be less than functional, and attendees were visibly disengaged.

Or I could decide otherwise. Instead, I chose to apply an adage that a Chicago screen acting instructor once taught me, and I've applied every day since. It was initially shared with me in the context of acting but is still applicable to other situations. She taught our class to *never play the victim*. What this means is that you never make excuses to justify poor performance.

For example, even though you arrive at an audition and are not given a script to prepare – even though you were told you would receive one – you still figure out a way to deliver your best performance. Or if the audition room is changed at the last minute, or you're called in to audition first when you were told you were last, or they request you do a cold read with a new script when you were asked to prepare a different one, you never make excuses. No matter what comes your way or what limitations you face, you find a way to do your best. Period.

In San Antonio, I realized I'd flown all the way across the country to be away from my family and home. So, to make that sacrifice worth it, I decided to commit to doing everything in my power to teach this audience presentation skills – with or without workbooks. Somehow, I would find a way to make this work. I would not *play the victim*. So, I set my intention that by the end of the day – no matter what – these customers would be better public speakers than when they first arrived. I committed to giving 110%. And that inner commitment changed everything.

As I waited off to the side of the room, I took a deep breath and heard myself being introduced. I made my way to the front. I knew I had to bring positivity and fun quickly. I welcomed them with as much energy as I could and asked if they would be willing to leave their seats at the back of the room and find chairs at tables near the front instead. Their collective answer stunned me. They said no. But I knew that less distance between us was essential for connection. So, I asked, 'Are you willing to slide your current chairs to the front of the room instead?' Thankfully, they agreed.

As the day progressed, I discovered a new freedom which liberated me from the structure of a facilitator guide and participant workbooks. I went along with the flow of what was happening for learners in the room and even created some activities for them on the fly that were not in the workbooks.

For example, some of them shared with me that they were deathly afraid to speak in front of others, so I brought them up to the front one-by-one. I asked them to sit in a chair in front of their peers, and then I sat in a chair next to them to offer support and share the spotlight. I asked them about their favorite hobbies, and we had a conversation about it while their colleagues watched in the audience. Everyone laughed and we were all engaged. It wasn't a speech; it was a conversation about a topic they loved. Strategically, I was warming them up to feel more comfortable speaking in front of others, as we inched our way toward skill improvement.

As the training day progressed, they continued to practice their skills by introducing themselves in front of the audience. I welcomed positive feedback from all participants about what each speaker was doing well. And then I offered constructive feedback for improvement with live coaching. This gave them the opportunity to practice, receive feedback, and then do it again. They continued to improve, and their faces lit up as they observed their confidence growing. They could also feel my commitment, and they could tell I wanted to make a difference for them.

Near the end of our time together, I remembered we had no formal evaluations. But applying the adage, I asked them to find pieces of paper in their own supplies or around the room to write down their feedback about the training experience. Years later, I still have those handwritten evaluations on torn half-sheets of paper. One evaluation reads, 'I learned more today about public speaking than in my semester class at college' or 'I can't believe how much I improved today!'

To close, I thanked them for their excellent participation and shared how proud I was of their accomplishments. Then something unbelievable happened. To my utter astonishment, I watched with amazement as the entire class of participants started applauding, and rose to their feet in a standing ovation!

In my decades of working with global training audiences, I've never experienced a training day that seemed so destined for disaster. Yet ironically, it was also the only training class where I received a standing ovation. That experience taught me that even when it looks like a flame is extinguished, the pilot light is still lit. You work with what you have and see where it goes. Most importantly, I learned to *never play the victim*. And it was because of this resilience that the day everything went wrong transformed into one of the best successes.

About Diana L. Howles

Diana L. Howles, MA, is an award-winning speaker, author, and global virtual and hybrid training expert who brings 25 years of experience in the learning industry. As a world-class facilitator, she has trained Fortune 100 and 500 companies, and facilitated virtual programs in more than a dozen countries! She is author of the Amazon best-selling book, *Next Level Virtual Training: Advance Your Facilitation*. Ms. Howles is currently CEO of Howles Associates, LLC, and is a popular speaker at international conferences and events. She can be reached via her website at www.howlesassociates.com or on LinkedIn.

Amazon Link to Diana's Debut Book - *https://lnkd.in/dttje6JE*

Facebook - *https://www.facebook.com/diana.howles*

LinkedIn - *https://www.linkedin.com/in/dianahowles*

Twitter - *https://twitter.com/dianahowles*

YouTube - *https://www.youtube.com/@dianal.howles2404/ videos*

Website - *https://howlesassociates.com*

Resilience For A Purpose

Estela Dalayoan-Pinlac, B.A., CEO

I wanted to start my chapter by being authentic and transparent. I procrastinated and overanalyzed writing this chapter because it is about me. The truth is I'm afraid of being vulnerable to share my story because it may not be 'good enough.'

My name is Maria Estela Dalayoan-Pinlac, and I am making a difference this time for me. I am stepping into the light, to share my voice, my big dreams, and to celebrate all the wins that I am grateful to have experienced, because growing up, I didn't really celebrate the milestones. Although I did well in school, selected into the 1st International Baccalaureate Program at Sisler High School and received academic awards, I always felt it wasn't enough. I found myself more interested in school activities and sports because I enjoyed being part of a team.

'There are no shortcuts to any place worth going.'
Beverly Sills

As an immigrant, I didn't know who I was and the tribe I belonged to. I never shared with anyone how I was bullied and chased home by two girls on a regular basis in elementary school. My black hair was yanked during classes, and I was teased for my 'slanted eyes' and my cavity infested teeth. However, I was constantly told that I had to assimilate into this new world that didn't welcome me or wanted me. This was my first experience of rejection and feeling of being 'not good enough'.

Personally and professionally, I felt many times 'not good enough'. Only recently, I realized that the absence of support and validation from a tribe can impact ones' growth and can leave invisible scars. This is why I strive and I am driven to ensure that every child and every person should feel welcomed and feel they belong.

Finding My Tribe But Not My Purpose

When I was thirteen years old, our parents wanted us to learn more about our Filipino heritage and not lose our Filipino culture, that was when my brothers and I joined Magdaragat, a Filipino Performing Dance Ensemble. This was when I discovered my cultural identity, and I found my tribe who made me feel I belonged. Being part of this tribe, I learnt to face my fears of not belonging, I became more confident, and proud of being Filipino.

We performed for the Royal Visits, annual Folkorama events, at Disney World Epcot Centre, but the 74th Inter-Parliamentary Union Assembly performance in Ottawa (1985) impacted me the most. I was inspired to become an international delegate so I can make a difference in the world. I began facilitating youth workshops, volunteered for Members of Parliament Constituency offices, and attended youth conferences. I recall participating at the Tri-National Youth Conference held in Montreal, where delegates from the Filipino, Indian, and Chinese communities across Canada shared common challenges the youths faced. I shared my learnings of the cultural identity crisis that immigrant youths experienced as they navigate in society as a Canadian, balancing their cultural identities while at home, respecting the old traditions of their parents and heritage. At that moment, I thought I found my purpose.

As soon as I graduated from University of Winnipeg in 1994 with a Bachelor of Arts Degree, Majors in Political Science and Canadian History, I moved to Toronto to attain a Public Relations Certificate at Ryerson Polytechnic University. I also accepted a contract position at North York University to assist with coordinating the 1st United Nations Youth Forum. It was an amazing and rewarding experience to coordinate volunteers and 500 youths attending the first UN Youth Forum representing their countries. It was a once in a lifetime opportunity for these youths to share the challenges they face, find commonalities, to learn from each other, and to collaborate. The UN Youth

Forum was a success, however, my experience was bittersweet. My rosy coloured glasses were shattered. I couldn't continue to hide the disappointment of working for a person who did not have the values and respect for others. This finally made me realize I didn't have the resiliency to stay because this was not my purpose.

From The Dark, I Found Purpose

For a few years I felt lost, however in the summer of 1996, Arthur and I decided to move to Calgary. By 1998 we got married, with both our careers in place, and a newly built home, we were ready to start a family and create our own tribe. Unfortunately, I was diagnosed with Polycystic Ovarian Syndrome (POS). For nearly six years of going to fertility clinics, taking medications, and even after several laparoscopies to remove the cysts, I was physically, emotionally, and mentally exhausted. It truly felt like riding a long rollercoaster ride that you wish was over.

By summer of 2003, Arthur and I decided to stop the fertility program and consider adoption, but my longing to build my own tribe was breaking me. One day, I fell to my knees and literally sobbing uncontrollably asking God for a child. I had pleaded and promised to love, protect, and raise a child equally and unconditionally without question.

In January 2004, a miracle happened, I was pregnant! My husband and I were over the moon with happiness.

However, my pregnancy only made it to 24 weeks and six days, I began to feel contractions, and was rushed to the hospital. It felt like an ER scene from a movie. I won't lie, it was scary but yet my unwavering faith in God made it easier for me to know everything was going to be fine, and it was. My beautiful baby girl was born weighing less than a pound. Within her first month, they performed a heart surgery, a laser eye surgery to prevent her from completely losing vision, and lastly, it was confirmed that she would have permanent severe profound hearing loss.

The amazing NICU team at Foothills Hospitals, took such great care of Madison for 91 days and when she reached the magic weight of 5lbs we were able to bring her home, even if she still required oxygen to support her breathing.

During one of many annual Doctors' assessment, we were told to be prepared that Madison would likely have up to a grade 8 equivalent learning capacity, and a slim chance of attending post-secondary education. Even her grade six teacher stated something very similar.

In June of 2022, she proved them wrong. Madison graduated with a Knowledge & Employability Certificate (K&E), and received the high achievement award for this program.

Madison overcame adversity and learned to self-advocate to remove communication and vision barriers, and pushed for her rights to access information.

She returned to school to finish two courses in order to receive her Grade 12 Diploma, giving her the option to attend a post-secondary education.

In 2007, our second miracle baby was born, Matthew who was born full term, with no complications. He is an active teenager, talented artist and loves to play hockey. Matthew constantly reminds me to balance life and to still remember to do the things that I love to do for myself.

As you can imagine, I have vested interest in making accessibility my top priority in order to ensure equal access for all is available. I understand the business hurdles, technology gaps, process challenges, and people's adoption obstacles that create the foundation of the brick wall that needs to be broken down. Which is why, in the last eight years, my big dream for some people may feel too big to deliver on. However, I believe, there is no dream big enough that can't be achieved when you have a well planned strategy, surrounded by experienced, passionate, and like-minded people to help make it happen; and most importantly, motivated by love. Love for our children, love for our community, for language, for innovation, for technology, and just love for a better World.

The pandemic woke me up to be courageous enough, vulnerable enough, to build a new company with my tribe. Make A Difference Through Inclusion Ltd (MADTI), is a social enterprise for-profit company with a mission to be the vessel to equalize communication access for all abilities.

To achieve this big dream, means to create a movement that is propelled by new innovation, new assistive technology, new governance, and new mindset. However, it must be willed by people at every level to remove ableism and support people with disabilities who have been and continue to be misunderstood, muted, unseen, forgotten, and often capped, because of barriers that still exist today.

Innovation for a purpose will continue to move forward because those that believe in the purpose will not allow it to fail.

Despite adversities and obstacles, I developed resilience and found my purpose. I am resilient because my children remind me that resiliency is a choice and the will to never give up when you have something worth fighting for.

'Purpose, grit, humility, and love are what will get me to the finish line.'

About Estela Dalayoan-Pinlac, B.A., CEO

In 1976, Estela and her family immigrated from the Philippines to Turtle Island, known as Canada to reunite with her father who she had never met since he left to work abroad for five years. She is the second youngest of the six children who grew up in Winnipeg, Manitoba  before she moved in 1996 to Calgary, Alberta.

Estela is a social entrepreneur, the CEO of Make A Difference Through Inclusion Ltd. (MADTI), and a Director and Founding member of Keywork Labs Inc. Her roles as a people leader, Strategic Business Advisor, Technology Innovation and Accessibility Consultant, and a mentor to start-ups are not as important to her as being a mother and wife. With a family of her own, she understands the sacrifices and the resilience her parents experienced to build a better life for the family. Estela's story is one of resilience, determination, and commitment to making a positive impact in the world.

linkedin.com/in/estelapinlac

www.madti.ca

It's Never Too Late To Achieve Your Dreams - One Woman's Journey Of Reinvention

Lisa Marie Gilbert, Author-Poet-Dreamer

From the age of five, abuse and neglect forced me to become a fighter and creative thinker in order to survive. Now, as a successful entrepreneur, author, wife and mother, I am a strong woman, a true survivor. This is the story of how belief in myself and the power of positivity helped me achieve my dreams.

My childhood was riddled with hardship, and I was no stranger to dealing with whatever nightmare came next. My father left us and divorced my mother when I was five, my mom had no real support, and it was always a battle to get even the minimal child support payment.

By the time I was 12, I was working at a gas station pumping gas and running the cash register to help my mother make mortgage payments. I remember having to run down to the gas or electric company several times to give whatever dollars in my pocket to beg them not to shut our heat or lights off. I remember having to steal napkins from the convenience store which we used as toilet paper or not having a single piece of food in our fridge or pantry other than my Grampa's canned tomatoes. Desperation, fear and defeat defined my mother's life as her daughters were witness to the men in her life walking all over her; negative lessons for a young lady to learn by the age of five.

My career started when I was 18 years old. My sister and I were recently orphaned when our mother passed away and our father abandoned us. We knew the only ones we could rely on was ourselves. I convinced my grandfather to let my sister stay with them, but I had to find somewhere to live and survive on my own. I quickly learned that the path that I thought my life would take was over. I would not be going to university to become a lawyer, teacher or writer. Nor was it likely that I would marry my knight in shining armor and have four children in the big house with the red door and white picket fence living happily ever after. Life had a different plan for me. Desperation and fear could have become my reality, but I made the choice that defeat would not be my life story. These hardships and tragedies were NOT going to define me like they did my mother.

I found employment at a wholesale distributor company working in the warehouse. The company had an established base and a great potential list of key contacts but had not really taken off. I was thrown into the deep end of the pool immediately but by being in survivor mode, I was up for the task and met every challenge head on until I had it mastered. An old soul and armed with intelligence and streets smarts, my supervisor quickly learned my abilities and potential were well above the order-picker position that I had been hired for. I would pick an order and pay attention to all that was going on around me, the purchasing, pricing, merchandising, creating planograms, and learning the importance of gross profit margin and overhead. I would volunteer to help with everything from accounts receivable calls to running salesman reports. I was a sponge that adapted to my surroundings quickly. What can save our company money? How can we increase production with our sales team and warehouse staff? All questions I intended on answering and more while learning the ins and outs of the corporate world. I was fighting for my life, I needed to show and quickly what I was capable of.

I worked my way up the ladder all the way to managing the office and the warehouse, becoming the VP of operations after just over one year, a title I still hold to this day. No one offered me the position; I took it by simply proving that I was the best person in the room for the job. My husband, the company owner, and I fell in love almost at first sight. He knew instantly I was well beyond my 18 years intellectually and we fit in every way right off the bat. For me it was such a breath of fresh air to be around a smart, sober, ambitious man that wanted the same things out of life as I did. We were unstoppable and made a great team.

My husband started this company with strictly automotive related items for your vehicle, things you would find in a convenience store, an air freshener or a glove or functional fluids or additives for your car. From the very beginning, I recognized the potential our company had and once my husband and I became a joint force a year after my start it was even more drive for me as it wasn't just about being great at my job this was now about building and growing a business and life with my family- for my family. Together we grew and built this successful company, and I am proud to say we have now been in business for 36 years, 26 of which I have been at the helm of the ship.

From board rooms to promotional business dinners to walking tradeshows I was always trying to find new ways to grow and build the business.

My goal was to diversify the company so that all our eggs were not in one basket, so to speak. Finding new and different products, outside our wheelhouse even, thinking outside the box was key. Tradeshows became invaluable ways to source new manufacturers and acquire new items. Novelty candy put us on the map as the first company in Canada to bring in candy spray which became a best seller instantly. You could never stand still for too long you have to constantly move with the changing times and new technology.

I could see that novelty candy was slowing down after a good run for about ten years as economies change and things are constantly evolving in this business, we are in.

'Chance favors the prepared mind.'
A motto by Louis Pasteur we all can live our lives by.

In 2006, we diversified yet again and became the fulfillment center and the provisioning office for the pay-as-you-go cell phone program for a major convenient store chain. Another example where we happened to be conversing with the product manager- he mentioned in passing he was trying to start a cell phone program and in that conversation - in that moment - chance favors the prepared mind, we became the company to launch that entire program which we still do to this day, over 15 years later.

I cannot stress enough what the importance of building a network has meant for our company 'A List of Key Contacts' is worth pure gold. If I had a dollar for every time a product manager left one leading company and showed up years later working for the competition, I'd be a rich woman!

We never, ever burn a bridge.

This sets our company apart from the others and a big reason why we have achieved longevity. Building a rapport with clients is not an easy task but is mandatory for success, period.

Knowing when to push and not to push is an artform that took time to master but if we are patient and pay attention to all around us, good things will come. For example, we wouldn't just go and take our one client out for dinner with his wife, we would stop by the office and make introductions and put our faces out there to all the people in the office. I can't tell you how many times this became an asset to us as product managers shifted around constantly. For example, the gentleman that you always included in your Christmas card list or invited to your company golf tournament ended up being your product manager two years later. At the time it might not seem important, but it sure becomes important later.

We were nice and charming to everyone we met, from the mail room or the field all the way up the ladder because we would never know where those good deeds would come back to help us later. I remember we took our product manager out for dinner, and he asked us at the last minute if he could bring along a field consultant that was staying in the same hotel as him. Of course, we said, the more the merrier (when we could not actually afford it). This field consultant ended up ten years later taking on the highest position in the company and ended up being that product manager's boss. He remembered that we took him out on that dinner and to this day that act of kindness and the laughs we shared that night have been the foundation of a great relationship.

Take an interest in all the surrounding people in

your field- learn names and family names -successful networking is everything in the corporate world.

Time flies when you're building a successful company - 17 years to be exact before I put on my favorite hat - we introduced the world to our firstborn son in 2013 - the ultimate dream come true for me. I had a very difficult childhood and worked hard in my life to recover and survive after my mother passed away. Nothing could have made me happier than finally having a child of my own. I am an old hippie girl, so my child's name had to be unique and special. I named him Rayne - I nicknamed him Raynebow because I always tell people that he saved my life in so many ways. He helped me find the sun -he will always be the color in my sky pushing out all the grey clouds.

Rayne changed the game for me. Being his mom made me wonder if I could also revisit some of my other 'unreachable' dreams. Even if everyone thought I was crazy and even if I had no support why couldn't I put on a different hat to see how it fit if it made me happy?

I have always had a passion for music and writing stories or poetry since I was a little girl. So naturally, when Rayne came along, I wrote him a lullaby and sang it to him every night and still do even to this day at nine years old. The lullaby was filled with all the hopes, dreams and wishes I had for him, I wanted everything for him that I never had growing up. Years passed but I felt compelled to share this lullaby with the world, so I started the journey of turning it into a children's book. It was my dream to be a published author and I decided that I was not going to give up until I made my dream come true.

It is a choice we must make - whether it is in business or love - persistence - none of us should ever give up and I believe it is never too late to go after our new dreams or old ones in my case.

I had never done anything like this before and had no idea what I was doing. I had to do the work, the research – put myself out there way out of my comfort zone.

Going back to my business roots, I started networking to find the answers and connections needed to publish my book. I even asked mothers at my son's soccer games - has anyone ever published a book before? Very quickly, one of the mothers said she had and connected me with a publisher. With some sketches (I had a friend do) in hand and my book on a USB drive I met with the publisher. I was introduced to a book illustration artist, and we hit it off immediately. We started the journey of turning my words and my friend's sketches into my children's book. I had already decided on the characters – they had to be elephants with a hippie touch because they are special to me.

From start to finish the book process took about four years. Expensive mistakes were made, I admit, but I learned and gained so much from the experience. My very first children's book was published, a true legacy piece for my son and I. 'Mama's Words of

Wisdom' was launched September of 2021. Loading the book to Amazon was thrilling.

Sixty-hour work weeks plus being a full-time mama and publishing issues almost made me give up, but I never did. I stayed the course, and I am still going. It is important to try to stay positive, persistent and consistent with our goals. It was challenging to block out all the negative energy, but I am walking proof that you can achieve your dreams and it is never too late.

Self-publishing is not just writing the words, you also must find your audience. Using my networking business skills, I called bookstores, sold myself and my book to anyone who would listen. Before having a book, I was not on social media at all. Today I have a website, Instagram and Facebook pages and I believe all those things are important building blocks for my brand. I have come so far from the girl who is still listening to cassette tapes. I even appeared on a television show to promote my book. It was far out of my comfort zone but what an experience.

I kept putting myself out there and as my Mama used to say, *'If at first you don't succeed... try, try again.'* No one is going to bring my ship in for me I must swim out and get it. Putting in my time with phone calls and book signings, building new networks, keeping my eyes and ears open is paying off. I called my local newspaper and just flat out asked them if they would be willing to feature me and my book and they said yes. That was very exciting to be in a newspaper and of course I got a lot of exposure as a result which was great. But if I don't make the phone call and put myself out there that never would've happened. We were out for dinner one evening, I got a lead from the server that her mother worked in the children's department at the local library- talk about chance favors the prepared mind! I called them up and she loved my back story and the book - they created an entirely new event called a Mother's Day tea just for me - if I don't network and put myself out there that never would've happened.

I am currently working on trying to get my book listed with big box stores. One phone call led to another, but I wasn't getting any callbacks. Using my business skills, I befriended the secretary who, seeing my friendly persistence, helped me get a meeting with a buyer. I do not give up, even if the door is shut, I will knock and open it again.

We welcomed our second baby boy into our family - Mr. River - AKA Moonlight or River baby love. I prayed to God for him in one of my darkest hours and when he came into our life, I swear God sent him to me to give me a hug - he's the best cuddle bug in the world! Of course, I had to write a book for him too and so in the wee hours of the night in between feedings and work I wrote him a lullaby which I also turned into the second book of the Mama series called 'Mama's Pearls of Guidance'.

I really feel like my dream has come true.

As women, we must overcome many obstacles in this man's world we live in. I have overcome many trials and tribulations, but I never gave up and I wouldn't trade any of it because it has made me the wiser person I am today. A young girl who test reads my books asked, "When are you going to write one for a little girl?" I have so much to tell little girls, pieces of advice, pearls of wisdom. I decided to turn my mama series into a trilogy -the third and final book will be for all the little ladies out there.

Constantly asking questions – evolving with the times - growing my website with selling other merchandise or asking my editor how do I get more traffic on my website? She offered 'you can get some external traffic starting a blog' - switching gears throwing on another new hat - another passion of mine is to cook - I started a cooking blog on my website and this has gained new awareness and traffic and made me so happy - a win-win.

If I could go back in time, I would tell my 18-year-old self (with five dollars in her bank account) that all will be OK one day, and she will reach the mountain top. At 18, I would not have believed it, but it might have saved all those premature grey hairs!

I hope by leading by example my sons grow up to learn that they can do anything they want to do, that they need to dream until they make their dreams come true. There would never be a rainbow without the rain. 'Find the color in your sky and keep the sunshine in your pocket' I always tell them.

We must work at happiness - we must choose to be happy and to fight for what we believe in. I have faith in the Lord above that my journey will lead to success and happiness.

I have accepted change and reinvented myself several times over the course of life and I am proud to say my closet is full of many different, beautiful hats! Positive energy and persistence – we get what we give to this universe- we can do anything we put our minds to. Do you see the light? Build your own tunnel. Persevere my fellow ladies. We are women here us roar!

God Bless you all.

Love Mama Lisa Marie xoxoxox

About Lisa Marie Gilbert

Lisa Gilbert is an entrepreneur, wife and mother to two beautiful boys, but most of all she is a fighter and a true survivor. Lisa is walking proof that hard work, persistence, and networking can give you the power to make new and old dreams come true. In partnership with her husband, Lisa, as VP Operations has built a successful wholesale distributor company that is still growing after 36 years. Belief in herself and her resilience to rise above negative energy is what has been the key to Lisa's success.

After the birth of her first son Rayne, Lisa realized that she could dream new dreams, that it was never too late for reinvention. With her signature tenacity, while continuing in her existing roles, Lisa became a published children's book author. 'Mama's Words of Wisdom' is available on her website and Amazon, Indigo/Chapters, Barnes and Noble.

Compelled to write another book for her second son, River, Lisa's writing journey continued with the publishing of 'Mama's Pearls of Guidance'.

Lisa is currently in the process of writing the third book to complete the "Mama" series -an ode to all the strong women who have paved the way, and a heartfelt invitation to all the daughters of the world to always be true to themselves.

Stay tuned for 'Mama's Girl Guide to Believing in Yourself'.

From boardrooms to playdates to book signings, Lisa proves you can reinvent yourself and accomplish anything you put your mind to.

Connect with Lisa and follow along on her magical carpet ride at all the sites below:

www.lisamarie-gilbert.com

www.facebook.com/lisamariegilbertwriter

www.instagram.com/lisagilbert_author

www.calaltasupplyltd.com

www.blazoninternational.ca

Overcoming Self Doubt Saved My Life

Shenneile Henry

My life changed forever one night in the shower after a stressful week. What I had hoped to be a relaxing evening quickly turned into a moment that led me to see my life flashed before my eyes and my neighbour having to call 911.

I was wrapping up my evening and taking a shower. I had been coping with a lot of individuals, on a mission to paint me as something I am not - selfish, a bully, out of control, unfit, unreliable, uncoachable, not-fitting-in, aggressive Black woman. It wasn't one time occurrences, but repeated, intentional and deliberate actions by friends and colleagues masked as 'family', which went on for a long time that started to consume my life. Their distaste towards me when I shared good news like purchasing my first home or getting a promotion would turn their smiles into frowns and was visibly upsetting news for them.

The negative labels placed on me were constantly on my mind, consuming my everyday thoughts, my everyday decisions, and ultimately consuming me. I was constantly hearing these labels and voices in my head on repeat like a megaphone.

The warm shower water trickled through my hair and down my face, my back was hurting from having been sitting at my computer all day. I was tired, looking forward to decompressing for the evening, but I started to ruminate on my week and life in general, my thoughts filled with a painful swirl of bad experiences.

As the water continued to flow over my hair, my face, and my body, the warm water started to feel like pins and needles hitting my skin. I reached down to adjust the temperature setting when I felt my entire body go numb. When I put my hand on my chest, it was as though my body did not exist - I felt nothing. I had completely lost my sense of touch.

Black and silver sparks filled my vision, I could make no sense of anything that was happening to me. I felt as though my chest was about to explode. My time had come, I thought. I was having a heart attack. It did not for a second occur to me that I was having a panic attack. Inside the moment, I believed I was having a heart attack, blacking out and on my final stretch of life. It was my family and the people that mattered most to me that came top of mind.

Gasping for air, I somehow managed to make my way to the balcony door. Laying half out the door despite it being below zero degrees, I tried to control my breathing. Once able, I called my neighbour who came downstairs and phoned the police for me.

The paramedics walked me through some breathing exercises that helped me come back to reality. With thought and reflection, it became clear to me that I had been so deep in thought of the negativity in my environment and under so much stress that my body had propelled itself into a state of panic trying to protect me from the feeling and fear of being lost; trapped.

For many years, I was living behind a curtain, afraid of showing up as who I am and how I want to be in this world. As someone who has volunteered nationally and overseas educating business owners in financial literacy and advising entrepreneurs on their business plans, I found great satisfaction supporting and extending myself to the community. I have always wanted to start my own business, but lacked the confidence to start myself. I felt a combination of guilt, shame and worthlessness; constantly questioning myself, expertise and my reality, which was distorted from being psychologically manipulated by the people around me - triggering my anxiety.

Early in my life, I was bullied for my being overweight, too dark, and my Jamaican accent.

In high school a group of guys told me they never aspire to marry a dark skinned girl. I used to wear oversized sweaters and baggy pants to hide my curves. I hated my body. I hated this dark-skinned, chubby girl from Jamaica. I yearned for adulthood, surely things would be different.

The sweet innocence of youth was sadly awakened to the realities of being an adult. In addition to being bullied because of my body, I was seen as being too reserved and quiet, labelled as 'that shy girl'. I tried to gain acceptance by pushing myself beyond my comfort zone to socialize and be more talkative. This only meant I hit a different wall of disapproval for being a 'social butterfly'. As I gained footing in the business and professional world, I was labelled aggressive for being ambitious. I would enter rooms with a bright smile on my face, not afraid to introduce myself to senior executives and award-winning business owners, I would hear whispers from people saying things like *'who does she think she is - Beyoncé?!'* followed by snarks and eye rolls directed towards me. It felt familiar like I was back to being that insecure chubby dark skinned girl. How would I navigate this? Over time I became afraid to introduce myself in rooms. I went back to filtering myself.

I often felt like the elephant in the room. Consistently taking up too much space.

I began to believe I did not belong.

Coupled with the fact that I have often found myself in spaces where I am the 'only' woman, Black woman, young person in the room, I found it easy to believe I was the problem. Other times because I was directly told 'you are not welcome here'.

It is safe to say that I lost myself.

I started to lose my appetite and sleep, my hair started falling out, and that is when my alarm bells went off. I had no good option but to make serious changes. After spending endless hours getting to know myself - meditating, travelling and reading various books, I had a 180 degree shift in my mindset which ultimately led to the start of my own consulting business.

If you have dealt with anxiety and have felt as though you are losing yourself, you know that it is not just 'being worried' or 'overthinking'. For me, anxiety is the mental and physical feeling that I am about to die. In the moment of a panic attack, I have no conscious awareness of what is actually happening - in that moment, I forget what a panic attack even is.

Having frequent panic attacks has been my reality for many years.

Having trained in the gym and listened to many podcasts, I got validation knowing that there are ways to cope.

There is power in storytelling, for me, I have found myself one too many times overthinking and underestimating the value of my story and voice. I've had negative self-talk to the point where I've talked myself out of doing things I know would bring me joy.

There was a turning point in my life that arose one day as I found myself laying in bed, staring at the roof in the dark, pondering on several questions:

Why was I so problematic?

Why do I make so many people uncomfortable?

I got out of bed, and turned on the lights in the bathroom.

I stared at my reflection in the mirror for a few seconds and said a few affirmations:

- I am one of a kind

- I am fearless

I then asked myself, *'Why do I care? They don't know ME.'*

Not only was I mentally tired, my body had physically spoken to me through anxiety and panic. After the shower day I made a personal vow to live life for me. Having dealt with bullies almost all my life has given me clarity on who I really am. The beliefs of others consumed my mind to the point where I was mentally and physically blocked, restricted. The person I am - giving, selfless, a lifelong learner, a person who believes the sky is not the limit, but the starting point, had given up her power to individuals who instead of getting to know her had created a false version of her in their heads.

Knowing who you are and what you bring to the table, owning it confidently and unapologetically is Power. MY Power! How I walk, talk, speak of myself, eat my favourite meals, wear what makes me comfortable is Power. Once you overcome self doubt, doing the things you love start to feel shame and guilt free.

The Stoic Philosopher, Marcus Aurealius said, *'You have power over your mind - not outside events. Realise this, and you will find strength,'* and *'The happiness of your life depends upon the quality of your thoughts'*.

I believe and have learned first hand that this is true.

What transpired from my shower that evening taught me the power my mind has over my life. This led me to starting my consulting business rooted in mindset coaching, education and confidence building. My brand represents me, and is for people who have or desire to have the smarts, integrity and passion to live life on their terms, people who seek to better their life and the lives of those around them.

My wish is to share my story with that individual, little girl or woman who feels they are on an island alone, who is self-doubting and being told they have no place in this world and business. If this is you, I hope this gives you the encouragement and validation to know there IS a place for you, anywhere you want to be in this world, so long as you believe in yourself.

About Shenneile Henry

Shenneile Henry is a proud Jamaican-Canadian woman. Having faced many roadblocks from childhood into adulthood, Shenneile can speak first hand to the saying 'rejection is merely a redirection; a course correction to your destiny' (McGill). Shenneile is known to challenge the status quo  and overcame many rejections to pave a successful path for herself and family in Finance, Real Estate and Entrepreneurship.

Also known as GOAL Digger Shen, Shenneile provides consulting services to business owners looking to start and grow their business(es). She was the 2022 recipient of the Under 30 Achievement Award presented by the Calgary Black Chambers and 2023 Women of Inspiration Nominee for her commitment as a leader in the Canada business community. Shenneile is a former Commercial Banker providing business owners with risk advisory services and loans up to 25 million dollars. She is the former President and current Strategic Advisor for non profit organization Young Women in Business, and is a Director for DirectHer Network whose mission is to see more women in boardrooms.

Email: *info@goaldiggershen.com*

Instagram: *https://www.instagram.com/goaldiggershen/*

Linkedin: *https://www.linkedin.com/in/goaldiggershen/*

Linktree: *https://linktr.ee/goaldiggershen* to book a free virtual coffee chat with me

Breaking the Shackles Of Paycheck Dependence - The Windy Road To Financial Freedom In Real Estate

Whitney Elkins-Hutten, PhD, MPH

Have you ever started a business or side hustle and wondered if you will achieve financial freedom? I asked myself that same question multiple times before I succeeded in a field I never expected. Let me tell you the story of how I went from being a paycheck-dependent corporate employee to a financially free business owner, and you can too.

When I graduated with my Masters, I continued the path that society (and my parents) expected of me. I got a great paying job in community health, bought a house, got married, had a kid, and stuffed money away in my retirement accounts in hopes that one day I could retire.

Over the next few years, I succeeded quickly and found myself scaling the corporate ladder: first in training and development for a retail chain pharmacy, then in sales operations at a technology company. With each new promotion, I was charged with solving new business challenges, my title elevated, and my paycheck grew. Moreover, I thrived on being an intrapreneur as my parents said that being an entrepreneur was 'just too risky'.

Life was awesome. Except for one little (yet massive to me) problem: I lacked freedom.

Like many C-suite professionals, I was expected to be at my job all hours of the day plus weekends and travel on a moment's notice. I was juggling these crippling expectations all while trying to maintain my relationship with my husband, raise a newborn baby girl and care for elderly family members.

Burning the candle at both ends and five times in the middle was practically a norm.

And even if I had worked eighty plus hours the week before away from my family and wanted a couple of hours to attend my daughter's school events, I had to submit a time-off request.

That really made me incredibly frustrated.

You see, years before, I watched my father struggle with Parkinson's disease to the point he was completely debilitated. He too was a C-suite executive, trading his life for a paycheck and significance, in hopes of one day retiring 'rich'. As his health deteriorated, it became abundantly clear to me that time was a precious and non-renewable resource.

In my corporate 'dream job' that I was giving every ounce of my being to, I had money, but I didn't have my most precious resource - my time. I was shackled by the golden handcuffs of paycheck dependence and employment security.

One night in my hotel room, weary from a long day of business travel, I wondered how I could get my time back and continue scaling my income? I had the business skills, so why not put those skills to use for me and mine?

Desperate for a path to freedom, I scoured the internet, reading scores of blog posts, about individuals leaving their jobs after achieving 'financial independence (FIRE)' and discovered their go-to books were *Rich Dad, Poor Dad* by Robert Kiyosaki, and *The Automatic Millionaire* by David Bach.

After downloading and devouring both books, both gurus said the same thing - that real estate was *'The Thing'* that made more ordinary people millionaires (and billionaires) and helped them exit the 'rat race' now... not in thirty to forty years.

I was sold! I opened my real estate investing business the next week and committed what was left of my nights and weekends to growing this business as quickly possible so I could leave the corporate world and be with my family.

I did just that - scaling my rental portfolio to over thirty single-family properties in a short eighteen months and bringing home a high five-figure, tax-free income with massive upside potential. Not too shabby.

But the reality was sinking in.

Although I had scaled my real estate business to where I could leave my corporate job. I found myself working almost as many hours - managing lenders, property managers, construction timelines, and tenants. To compound the issue, while I may have been able to leave nine to five JOB life, we needed more than eighty homes to get my husband out of his work in order to fully embrace financial freedom as a family.

The time freedom and financial freedom I desired was eluding me. For the first time in years, I had a glimmer of hope that I might be on the right track of scaling a business for myself, but I still hadn't figured out how to make reliable cashflow in my sleep (the holy grail that every business owner dreams of).

Then, just as I was gaining momentum in growing my portfolio, I was laid off right before Christmas. The paycheck was now gone.

At first, I felt every emotion you might expect from someone who just lost their job. But that lasted a few short hours because, for the first time in eleven years,

I didn't have to ask for time off during the holidays. I could be with family and travel whenever and wherever we wanted.

True, I still had to manage my investing business from the road, but I could see and touch the life I wanted. For the first time in years, I could attend my daughter's holiday performance, sleep in on Christmas Eve, and take a last minute New Year's trip to the East Coast, all without having to put in a time-off request and cross my fingers it would get approved. I knew it was 'now or never'. I had to figure out how to scale my real estate investing business NOW.

So how did I do it? Well, I would like to say that I just bought a piece of real estate, then another, and another and another and I rode off into the sunset. But that is not what happened. I was still gripped by fear and self-doubt that I could actually achieve my goal of financial freedom. To get to the bottom of this, I had to ask myself two massively important questions: *What do I want? Why do I want it?*

If I messed up this step, I knew I would scale a real estate business that I would hate to own later. Clarity is power, my friends. I knew I wanted to own a business that gave me financial freedom, time freedom, freedom of choice, and freedom of location. Where I no longer had to trade time for money, and where my investments would 100% cover my expenses and my desired lifestyle. Not because I want to lay on the beach all day (which I suck at BTW), but to allow me to go and create the impact in the world that I am born to create.

That meant I needed to invest in stabilized assets that cash flowed well now, assets where the valuation growth was not left to chance, and where I was not the day-to-day operator of the asset so I could have my time back and be free to travel.

The natural investment choice was multifamily buildings. I could get five or more units with each transaction (though my ideal purchase would be one hundred or more units), stabilized cashflow because I now had multiple tenants covering the expenses, and better property management. Just one tiny problem - I didn't have any experience purchasing a multifamily building.

Did I even want to own the building? Or was there a way I could invest in someone else's building? Now for the hardest question - who did I need to become to get what I wanted? In order to get what I wanted want, I needed three key ingredients - mindset, skills, and networks.

First, I first had to deal with my **mindset.**

- I needed to understand my life priorities and align them with my daily actions. While I did take a 'detour' by investing in active real estate projects, tuning into my 'what and why' informed me that 90% of my focus needed to be on finding ways to invest in other people's projects i.e., passive investing).

- I needed to overcome my limiting beliefs (those stories I told myself when things weren't going my way). Any one of these thoughts would undermine my momentum and success.

  - I don't have time, or it is too hard to re-engineer this investing business.

  - I don't have the money to invest in larger assets.

  - I don't deserve this.

Next, I needed to update my **skills toolbox.**

- I needed to learn how to reverse engineer my goals and create consistent and persistent action – making the investing steps so small and achievable that I could not fail.

- I needed a system – to find great businesspeople to invest with, in the best real estate markets, and a sure-fire way to underwrite passive deals to protect my capital and mitigate risk.

Last, I needed a **team** of the brightest and most experienced real estate operators I could find to help me achieve my financial goals.

Fast forward almost seven years. I have solved each one of the challenge areas above and recreated my passive real estate investing business focused on truly passive income the only way I knew how - I invested in one passive real estate investment.

Then another. And another. And another. Then the flywheel on my new passive real estate business began to spin. Cashflow started to compound, exits started to happen, and our portfolio doubled not once but twice. Now, the money that comes in while I am sleeping/traveling/running is more than enough to support myself and my family for the rest of our lives. My husband no longer thinks I am nuts.

That is true freedom. I still work, I love my work. And I get to choose the impact I want to create in the world. I have broken the shackles of paycheck dependence because at the end of the day what we all really want is freedom to do what we want, when we want, with whom we want.

Here at *PassiveInvestingWithWhitney.com*, I want to show you how I got here — and help you do the same. Join me at our online community that's helping people just like you build true financial freedom.

About Whitney Elkins-Hutten

Whitney is the Director of Investor Education at PassiveInvesting. com, a national passive real estate investment firm that has acquired 3,300+ multifamily units, 6,600+ self-storage units, seventeen car washes, and 153 hotel keys with a portfolio valued at over $1.3B with over 2,000  investors active in those assets. She is also the host of the Passive Investing Made Simple YouTube Show and Podcast.

Whitney stumbled into real estate by accident. After purchasing her first rental in 2002, and hitting a home run, then nearly losing it all on her second deal, she took control and figured out how to invest in real estate the right way; replicating the very personal finance and wealth creation strategies the wealthy use to create financial freedom.

Today, Whitney is a partner in $800MM+ in real estate — including over 6500+ residential units, seven express car washes, and more than 2200+ self-storage units across eleven states—and has experience flipping over $5.0MM in residential real estate.

Email: *Whitney@passiveinvesting.com*

Website: *https://www.passiveinvesting.com/*

LinkedIn: *https://www.linkedin.com/inwhitneyelkinshutten/*

Building Resilience:
How Leaders Can Prepare For
And Thrive In A Changing World

Kylie Denton

As someone that develops leaders each day, I am often
asked by organisations to help develop their leaders
into *resilient leaders.*

I remind them that resilient leadership isn't a
presentation that we just run and an hour later you
have resilient leaders. Developing resilient leaders is
a process.

Resilient leadership refers to a leaders ability to work
through challenges, adapt to changes, get back up after
setbacks and inspire their people and guide their teams
to do the same.

Resilient leaders are looking for or anticipating future
challenges, they are visionary, they are not sitting still

and waiting for something to happen they are proactive, they know that nothing stays the same. They remain calm under pressure, they help others to see the future and they inspire confidence and motivation to those around them.

Resilient leaders learn from their mistakes, they understand that failure is feedback and they know that through this failure they will grow and improve.

Resilient leaders are optimistic in the face of adversity and they inspire that optimism in others.

As you can see resilient leadership is a comprehensive program that encompasses a wide range of skills and competencies aimed at building resilience. As a result of this I focus on developing various skills and competencies to help them become more resilient and effective leaders.

Although I would love to be able to share with you all the skills and competencies you need to develop resilience in one chapter it is impossible, however I want to share with you at least eight distinct areas that will help you begin building your resilience as a leader.

Failure

Resilient leaders understand that failure is inevitable and they don't see it as a reflection of their abilities but they see it as an opportunity to grow and improve.

Failure helps us to adjust our strategies, learn, and move forward with greater clarity and confidence. Lewis Howes an entrepreneur often says that failure is just feedback. I know as a business owner that I see failure as a learning. Learning what not to do but also learning what to do differently next time. Without failure I wouldn't be where I am today. Does it feel good to fail, no I would be kidding if I said it did, but resilience comes from when we get back up and learn from failure that makes me (us) stronger. How are you learning from your failings?

Confidence

We know this is an important trait for any leader. Confidence in the context of resilient leadership is believing in your own ability to navigate challenges and move forward even when there are setbacks and unknowns. Resilient leaders maintain this confidence even when things don't go as planned. Confident resilient leaders know they don't have all the answers and they seek help and input from others which helps them maintain that sense of confidence. What steps are you taking to build your confidence?

Collaborate

Resilient leaders collaborate. Collaboration helps us to achieve better outcomes as it leverages different perspectives. When we work together in collaboration, we harness the collective intelligence of the group.

Uncovering and utilising their skills and experience. No one person can have all the answers, when we collaborate, we generate new ideas, see our blind spots and increase our chance of finding successful solutions. Collaboration builds resilience not only in the leader but also in the team as they are learning how to make decisions, solve problems and work as a team, they are in fact learning how to collaborate. Collaborating with your people means they feel like they have some control over the direction of the business. Who should you be collaborating with and how will you go about it?

Decisiveness

Resilient leaders are able to make informed decisions in a timely manner. They know that delayed decisions can create new problems or exacerbate problems. It's important to note that I am not saying making quick decisions I am saying resilient leaders understand the importance of balancing speed with quality information. Resilient leaders also pivot and adapt their decisions based on new information or changes in circumstances. They don't make a decision and stick to it, if it needs to be changed, they change it. Resilient leaders are balanced, and adaptable when it comes to decision making, they are agile and flexible in order to achieve successful outcomes.

Focus

Our world is full of distractions - everywhere. And it takes a real effort to stay committed and focused. Resilient leaders maintain a clear sense of purpose and direction even in the face of uncertainty. They prioritise and focus on the goal or the outcome. They have a very clear sense of vision and mission and that helps them to stay on track to achieve their goals even in the face of adversity or setback. How are you maintaining your focus?

Positive mindset

Resilient leaders have a positive mindset, this often helps them cope with challenges and setbacks. They don't dwell on problems or obstacles they find solutions and opportunities and look to the future.. Having a positive mindset is an important characteristic of resilient leadership. Having a positive mindset helps you to stay focused, motivated and adaptable, it also helps you to better cope. I understand that staying positive is not always easy in leadership but it is a key component of a resilient leader. Marcus Aurelius has a famous quote, The happiness of your life depends on the quality of your thoughts. There are many benefits to staying positive during uncertainty. How can you develop a positive mindset?

Belief

Resilient leaders believe in themselves. They know that self-belief is important not only for themselves but also for the people they lead. Resilient leaders believe in their abilities, they are self-aware of their own strengths and weaknesses, they know they can and will find solutions. Resilient leaders lean in, when others want to lean out and they believe that they can overcome any challenge or obstacle they face. They don't give up; they maintain that positive mindset and belief. What areas within yourself do you need to believe in more?

Empathy and understanding

Resilient leaders understand that results are achieved through people therefore they deal with the human element first. It's important that leaders demonstrate empathy and understanding that there are both personal and professional challenges that each of their people face. We shouldn't just assign this to human resources and feel we have done our part. We need to get in there and show these qualities ourselves. Although it is important, we show these qualities to our people, we also need to open ourselves up to receive empathy from others and to remain attentive to our own wellbeing.

Resilient leaders invest time into their own well so they can be resilient not only for themselves but the people around them.

Thank you for the opportunity to share with you some of the key aspects of resilient leadership. I hope this chapter has shown you that resilient leadership encompasses many different qualities and skills that leaders need in their tool box.

I've studied the habits and behaviors of the world's most successful leaders, such as Jack Welch, John Maxwell, Brian Tracey and Richard Branson and what I have learned is that there is not such thing as a natural born leader. Leadership is most definitely a skill which means that anyone can learn how to become a more resilient leader.

I can't emphasize the importance of resilience when it comes to leadership.

Leaders that build and develop resilience in their leadership are better able to navigate complexity, and challenges, they accept failures as feedback, they can cope with stress better, they are more adaptable to change, they make better decisions and focus on their goals, build a stronger and more resilient team whilst inspiring those around them.

Isn't that what true leaders really want? I know that is what I strive for.

About Kylie Denton

Kylie Denton is a bestselling author and highly experienced leadership consultant, professionally certified coach and speaker specialising in leadership and sales in the health, education government and financial services industry. With over thirty years' experience in Financial Services, and formal qualifications in psychology she has a proven track record and internationally recognised expertise in building confident leaders and successful teams. She has this innate ability to truly connect and understand her client's and is known for her ability to take people and organisations to the next level and turn good leaders into great leaders. Kylie pushes her coaching clients out of their comfort zone and challenges them to be the change they want to see in themselves and their business.

Kylie always has a wealth of information to share so reach out and connect

Kylie@performanceadvisorygroup.com.au

https://performanceadvisorygroup.com.au/

https://www.linkedin.com/in/kyliedenton5/

https://twitter.com/kyliedenton5

https://www.instagram.com/performanceadvisorygroup/

Escaping The Trap Of Perfectionism

Christine Cowern

I'm not entirely sure how or why I went from being a run-of-the-mill Type A personality to a full-blown burn-out perfectionist who couldn't sleep for fear of making the smallest mistake.

Maybe it was being the oldest child of a very successful, larger-than-life father – the kind of dad who went snorkelling in the Galapagos Islands with the same ease that he helped run multi-million-dollar businesses from Australia to Hong Kong. Or maybe it was a trait that I was born with, like my curiosity or impulsiveness.

Either way, when I started my real estate career in 2007, what I'd categorized up until then as nothing more than higher-than-average ambition, turned into more than ten years of self-imposed pressure and expectations so intense that they almost brought me –

and the real estate business I'd worked so hard to build – to our knees.

Masking my fraying nerves with lipstick and enthusiasm, it got to the point where I was dreaming almost every night of taking an extended vacation to any variety of sun-filled holiday towns where I could take leisurely walks on the beach and find as much sea glass as I could carry.

When I look back at the career success of both of my parents (my mom was equally accomplished in her own right), it's not a total surprise that I developed into the kind of kid who stressed out about homework and didn't want to raise her hand in class for fear of having the wrong answer. There was an unspoken expectation that we'd make something of ourselves, and that hard work was most definitely a prerequisite to succeed. And I was determined to do just that.

I was only a few months into real estate sales when my perfectionistic tendencies started rearing their ugly head. I'd recently joined a successful real estate team in my market area, one with flashy billboards, a slew of high-performing agents and a lot of internal and external pressure to succeed.

And boy, was I hell-bent on getting to the top. Hard work had gotten me continuous praise, job opportunities and higher salaries in the past, and I was completely convinced that it would do the same on my new team too. After all, why wouldn't it? I just had to work harder - and smarter - than everyone else.

I vividly remember sitting down in my first month on the team with a senior agent who'd been tasked with showing me the ropes. She didn't know what she was in for. For the next two hours, I peppered her with question after question on everything related to residential real estate sales (imagine a five-year-old fueled by sugar exhausting their teacher with every question they can think of). When we broke for lunch, I could see the palpable relief on her face that she could take a breather from her overly enthusiastic trainee.

If she was overwhelmed, you can imagine how I felt, acutely aware of not only my dwindling bank account but the fact that real estate is one of the most litigious industries in Canada, if not most countries. Not wanting to be on the other end of a lawsuit, I devoured everything I could find on representation, fiduciary duties, disclosures, warranties, and anything else that I decided I needed to know yesterday. Getting sued was not an option. I'd worked in careers with a lot of pressure before – like when I wrote the hourly news bites for a national broadcaster – but the pressure I was putting on myself this time felt different.

I became similarly obsessed with having the answer to every possible question a client could ask, writing contracts without so much as a misplaced comma and knowing every sale in every neighbourhood in my market area – you get the picture.

My workaholism quickly led to me cancelling social plans with alarming consistency, working every weekend, and often pulling 12-hour days, seven days a week. My friends, who were initially supportive, started calling me less often. It was like I was in a never-ending Groundhog Day, guzzling coffee and forgetting about life outside of my career goals.

What made my perfectionism even harder to navigate was that I was getting so highly rewarded for it. In the three years that I was part of the team, I rose from a lowly buyer's agent with the least amount of seniority and the fewest leads to the team's top listing agent. Given the competitive nature of the job, this wasn't an easy feat. My clients loved me too, giving me constant praise and business. My bank account had never been more robust, but I was increasingly stressed out and anxious at every turn.

Instead of noticing my increasing exhaustion and racing heart as important signs that something was wrong, I did the exact opposite and continued to reach for more. The next logical step in my mind was to build my own real estate team and so I left the team I was on and went out on my own as an independent agent, bringing on my first administrative assistant, then buyer's agent in quick succession.

On the outside, it looked like I had it made, but behind the scenes, my ambition and perfectionism were in a heated battle with each other, causing me to lose sleep nightly. My thoughts were often racing, and it wasn't uncommon for me to wake up at 3am, my mind spinning with thoughts like, *'You don't know enough'* or *'That wasn't done right.'*

My romantic relationships, if you can call them that, consisted of a few dates before the guy would get turned off by my constantly ringing phone. And I was lucky if I saw close friends a few times a year if that.

I realize now, looking back on it, that every time I up-levelled my career, the new pressures and skills I had to master took on a life of their own. Not content to just be 'okay' at any of it, I would create expectations for myself that were as high as Mount Everest around how many new clients I 'should' be working with or properties I 'should' be selling. At any moment feel like what I worked so hard to achieve could all come crumbling down.

I'd developed an intense fear of being judged or rejected because of 'mistakes' (ah, what a classic perfectionist trait!). It didn't help that those mistakes could have cost me a client or, worse, could have landed me in a lawsuit.

I remember being told the story of an agent who forgot to include a high-end washing machine and dryer in the inclusions for a property and having to pay out of pocket for them in full, to the tune of many hundreds of dollars. I was still thinking about it weeks later, anxious at the mere idea of making that kind of mistake and the possible repercussions.

Ironically, I was often praised by colleagues for my calm demeanour and ability to juggle an intense work schedule while appearing unruffled. I wasn't a big fan of mixing business with pleasure and kept a certain professional distance from my colleagues, so they weren't any wiser about what was going on with me behind the scenes. Little did they know how much my mental and physical health were suffering.

And all the while my real estate team grew – to four people, then five, then eight. And the external successes kept rolling in, which helped me justify my unhealthy trajectory. Year after year we won awards for sales production and were often featured in online articles, magazines, and TV segments, talking about everything from our take on the current real estate market to our rise to the top. With my demanding schedule and even more relentless inner critic, it was hard to enjoy all the accolades. I'd often acknowledge them in passing but then get right back to work.

By 2019, I was suffering from the classic signs of burnout: irritability, insomnia, and exhaustion. I'd made an appointment with a naturopath to try and get a handle on the physical symptoms of chronic stress that had started showing up in my body. When we sat down to go over the results, I found out that my cortisol levels – the primary stress hormone – were as high as if I was living in a battle zone.

It was beginning to dawn on me that there was something more going on than just having the drive to work hard. The last twelve years of operating at 110% all the time and expecting perfection had run me ragged. Even worse, I wasn't enjoying the career that I'd worked so tirelessly to build. In fact, I'd started to actively dislike it.

The thought came to me repeatedly: *'It's time to make a big change because I can't keep doing things this way.'*

One specific idea kept coming up again and again: quit real estate altogether. I'd started having regular daydreams about giving up the business and doing something completely different. Sitting in bed at night on my computer, I'd read stories about people who left their corporate jobs to start a bed and breakfast in another province or who had moved to Spain to escape the burnout culture that North America is so well-known for and thought, hey, maybe I can do that too.

Then realism would quickly set in. I thought about the time and energy (not to mention the money) that it would take to start all over again and decided there had to be a better way. My goal was to step away from working with clients in the field and create even more leverage for myself on the team so that I could get to the root of my perfectionism for good and create a noticeably more balanced life for myself.

'Get to the root of blocks, unleash potential and create real, sustainable change.' It was February 1, 2019, and the words I read on my computer screen leapt out at me. Over Christmas, I'd started searching online for a course or program that I could take to help me and within a week discovered a coaching organization online that seemed like exactly the right fit. They specialized in helping people become certified coaches in something called Energy Leadership ™.

I hadn't heard of it, but I was intrigued. I wasn't entirely sure that I wanted to get into coaching but, I thought, I'd always wanted to be of greater service so if this helps me and other realtors struggling with the same issues, it might be worth a try.

And so, in typical me fashion, I jumped right in. Within a week I had my offer of acceptance in hand and a month later I was sitting in a packed conference room in a hotel in the middle of downtown Toronto, not entirely sure what I was getting myself into but incredibly excited to start the process.

To call the program life-changing was an understatement. Over the course of the intensive three-month training, my mind was blown wide open to all the thoughts and beliefs I'd accumulated over time that were doing the opposite of serving me. The thoughts I assumed were the recipe for success were, in actual fact, robbing me of not only my true potential but my ability to have the best of both worlds – a thriving business and the work-life balance that I'd craved for so long.

What I was learning was that my long-held perfectionism had caused my brain to re-wire itself in ways that only added to the stress and pressure I'd constantly battled. Every perfection-focused thought had created a completely unsustainable environment in my brain and body. The constant barrage of thousands of conscious and unconscious thoughts explained the workaholic, perfectionistic challenges I'd been struggling with for years.

One of my most interesting discoveries was that there are different levels of energy we all operate within every day, from 1 being the lowest and most self-critical, to 7 being the highest and most empowering. If you think the same series of thoughts long enough, they'll turn into beliefs. Those beliefs will either keep you stressed out, anxious, defeated, frustrated, and stuck or on the completely other end of the spectrum, turn you into a resilient, empowered, focused, confident, energized, joy-filled person. The best part was that with practice you could stay at the highest levels of energy regardless of what was happening around you.

Wow. It was like an entirely new world had been opened for me – and it was my new path to take all the tools I'd learned and put them into action.

My first step was to do a deep dive into the racing thoughts and self-judgment I'd been plagued with for so long. I went to my local bookstore and bought a beautiful, leather-bound journal and started writing. I'd been a journalist and freelance writer in my past career, so the writing part came naturally to me, and it was so nice to put pen to paper again. It felt like I was going back to my roots.

It all came pouring out of me – I couldn't believe the negative, judgmental, critical thoughts that had been running my life for so long and the ridiculously high standards I'd used to measure my self-worth. As it turned out, there's a name for these kinds of thoughts – ANTs or automatic negative thoughts – and we're hardwired to have them because we've evolved as a species to constantly look for threats. Black and white thinking, being ruled by 'shoulds', taking things personally; I'd developed almost every single automatic negative thought there was over the years.

And I realized: because perfection is unattainable, in my quest to achieve it I'd literally caused my own anxiety and overwhelm. No one else, just me. It was a hard pill to swallow but it was liberating too because I knew that if I'd created the problem, I could also fix it.

Through conscious daily effort, I became acutely aware of what was going on in my brain. The first step was becoming conscious of the Level 1 thoughts I was having and the situations that triggered them. I realized that most of the stories I told myself, which all came filtered through the particular lens with which I viewed the world, weren't actually true.

I also realized that for years, and on a daily basis, I'd been experiencing the classic blocks that keep most people stuck in negative thinking loops, holding them back from seeing new opportunities and leading to a lot of self-sabotage.

The most powerful one was called a gremlin, that little voice in your head that's trying to protect you and keep you safe. For me, and I discovered for so many other perfectionists, it sounded like this: *'You're not good enough.'* When I believed that, to avoid what I perceived as possible judgment or blame, I tried to constantly meet my own made-up perceptions of what 'perfect' is.

Finally, figuring out my gremlin hit me like a ton of bricks. So that's why I'd been so hard on myself all those years and still didn't feel worthy regardless of everything I'd accomplished. It all started to make sense and I felt like a 200-pound weight had slowly started lifting off my shoulders.

I knew how many people, especially entrepreneurs and business owners who'd achieved success, likely struggled with the same perfectionistic beliefs that I did. No wonder there were so many people suffering from burnout or quitting their careers altogether for a simpler existence.

And that's when fate intervened. I'd just passed my coaching certification and was feeling a strong pull to start teaching people what I'd learned when one Monday, out of the blue, I got a call from a real estate colleague who I'd done a deal with many years earlier. After we caught up for a few minutes he told me that he wanted support growing his real estate business and that he was looking for a coach. 'Do you know of anyone?' he asked.

If I'd been looking for a sign, this was it. He became my first coaching client that day, one of many more to come. I kept thinking of the quote from American writer Richard Bach that you teach what you most need to learn. And a new chapter of my life began.

Fast forward four years later and my life looks very different than it did back then. I have a three-and-a-half-year-old son, who came into the world at almost the exact same time that I decided to change my life, and I'm the VP of Coaching & Development for an amazing coaching organization for realtors – a role that I absolutely love.

And yes, I'm still running my first baby – my real estate team – but in more of an operations and management role. The shift from being in the field to focusing on the team's long-term growth and success suits me to a tee. The icing on the cake? I'm the calmest, happiest, most fulfilled version of myself that I've ever been.

Don't get me wrong, I'm still ambitious and a hard worker, but when my perfectionism does start to show up – which happens so rarely now – I have the tools to immediately recognize it and let it go. Being free of the debilitating traps that plagued me for all those years, feels like a re-birth and I'm so grateful to be on the other side.

About Christine Cowern

Christine Cowern is the founder and managing partner of The Christine Cowern Real Estate Team, an all-female team of high-performing agents based in Toronto, Canada. Her team has been in the Top 1-2% based on sales volume since its inception in 2013 and has been featured on Global TV, CBC News and in the Globe & Mail, among other media.

A Certified Professional Coach with the Institute of Professional Excellence in Coaching, in 2022 Christine joined Endgame Coaching, an organization that helps Canadian realtors create 7-figure real estate businesses and teams. In her role as VP of Coaching & Development, she works closely with the Founder & CEO to drive growth, develop strategic partnerships, and attract, develop, and retain the best coaching talent.

A former journalist and television segment director, Christine holds a Master's in international journalism from City University in London, England. When she's not planning her next adventure, she's spending time with her son, husband and their cat Lily.

Instagram: *https://www.instagram.com/ realchristinecowern*

LinkedIn: *https://www.linkedin.com/in/christine-cowern*

You Are Already Capable And Already Resilient

Sheron Kenny

This article is for professional women who need to develop resilience, especially after a divorce.

How do you take care of yourself and be resilient under those sort of pressured, high stress conditions? It's actually easy when you become more aware.

When you are going through a divorce, you might not see what your own problems are and where you contributed to the problems until you come out the other end. Personally, I learned to stand up for my own values and giving kindness to myself.

It's when you start to understand your own inner strength, and concentrate purely on good intent, instead of allowing yourself to be at the affect by an ex-partner whom is negative and consuming your thinking.

I was in an abusive relationship at a young age and when I was in it, I often thought many times that I cannot cope, because of his behaviour. It took much strength and planning to leave and when I got out of that relationship, I slowly realized I *was* OK. I *could* do my own thing and not be controlled. If you allow yourself to be controlled, you cannot get on with your own life. I'm talking emotional growth, physical health, mental wellbeing and financial success.

I thought about taking back control of my life and that's what I did. I simply got on and concentrated with creating my own success. I had big dreams and great purpose to strive to be the best version of myself.

There were many challenges along the way and I developed the resilience to never give up.

To me everything's about listening to my awareness, my gut feelings that nudge and niggle at me, giving me a warning sign to take action. That's how we build resilience.

When you're in the middle of a separation and divorce its hard work, it consumes our thoughts, it affects our personal and professional lives. But when you finally step out of it, if you look back, you actually see your own strength and realise you can be your authentic self. Concentrate on what you need to do to succeed – not what anybody expects you to do. That's how I did it.

Change takes a lot of work when you're immersed in something emotionally painful – being triggered all the time and not thinking straight. At some point, you need to become aware that you are being triggered. When you feel triggered, ask yourself, what does feel like? When you become triggered by a simple gesture from a friend, ask, who's that about? ME. ME. ME. Notice that, especially when you first even come out of a relationship or a divorce, many day-to-day situations can feel challenging.

But everything we need is already within us, to be able to be strong.

Take note, we can choose to be weak and live in the past pain, or we can choose to say, *'Hang on, I need to think this through. I need to step back and see what's really going on here. And I don't need to be a victim.' I will be accountable for my own happiness.* Happiness is an inside job!

That was my thing. I chose never to be a victim, again. I took control of my own happiness, and I now do the things that give me happiness.

Self awareness. That's how we grow.

I developed the idea that when I've made a mistake, I take on the accountability and say, *Oh, I'll never do that again.* That's how you build resilience. I'm talking about awareness; and paying attention to your awareness. Such as, *I realised that person was abusive right at the start, but I ignored my inner gut instincts...* and then made excuses for staying.

I was chatting with a client who was emotionally upset and immersed in her feelings about her ex. She's 100% deep inside, dwelling in the pain. There's little awareness there - but not enough awareness, *I am getting upset.* She's just immersed and hating feeling so bad.

If you have actually exited the marriage and divorced notice if you are still emotionally caught up in it? There might be grief, of course, and many self-defeating doubts that consume your thinking such as the self-talk of *'I could have made that work better'. 'Was it really that bad?' 'Was it me?'* Doubting yourself with what-if's and but's. If you are thinking in the negative past, notice it. Change it to forward positive thinking of what you want now and in your future. Because you are worth valuing you whole mind, body and soul.

Past negative happens with a lot of women especially where children are involved. We all have to go through a grieving process. I don't think anybody wants to divorce and I don't think anybody wants to have anything bad happen in their life or to hurt others. Most people are decent human beings who don't want to bring pain to the other person. But even when it is a clean split, there's still going to be lots of emotions, sad feelings and doubts. *Did I do wrong thing? What could I have done better? Should I have tried harder for the kids?*

But notice that. Normalise doubts. Naturally you will second guess your choices and what happened.

But be aware that you are having doubts.

Notice them. Be mindful. You start to grow when you start to look in the longer term. And as you take action you grow and you become more resilient through your own awareness and accepting what happened. And then, by not being so hard on yourself. Sometimes, things just take time to heal but being kind to yourself aids the healing process.

You might still going through something which is quite difficult so there's a danger that you can over judge what happened then... and now. But as you become more aware you become more resilient and you might start to think, *Okay, it wasn't ideal, it wasn't a good thing, it was disappointing, it was stressful* but you're saying that with awareness.

What makes you resilient is an awareness of, *Okay, that was a challenging situation but what have I learned from it?* And then: *how am I going to grow from this and not make the same mistakes?*

I still experience challenges. Having these self-reflecting questions that I ask myself changes my thought pattern. *What do I need to grow in me? What will I do next time?*

Notice if you are upset. Have that awareness. Be upset. *Feel* those feelings, *feel* the pain but don't dwell on it for too long – get moving, even go for a walk and appreciate what's around you. Ensure to notice also if you are feeling like a victim. A lot of women are deeply immersed and reacting from being the victim without even realizing it. There's no awareness there.

There's something healthy about recognising, *Ah, sounds like I am a victim.*

Victim mentality puts you in a state of weakness – *poor me* thinking. That can happen easily, especially if you are constantly thinking, *I should have done this... I should have done that... I should have been a better person...* Notice that self-talk, that inner dialogue. Are you learning from self-talk or simply being self-disparaging or self-denigrating.

I talk to women that have been in a relationship that they know is not healthy for their self-esteem... they can *feel* it's no good... they *want* to get out of that relationship... and *know* they should get out... but they stay. They'll say, *I should have got out of it years ago... I've wasted my life* and become angry. The problem is they're not looking after themselves to stay in any situation that creates unhappiness. They stay there for the wrong reasons. And who wants to be in a loveless marriage? Nobody does. But it's up to them to get out of it and be true to oneself.

We all want love, nurturing and support, right? Sometimes, women think relationships have to last forever, regardless of the quality of that marriage. That is just our conditioning ruling our decisions. You get married... and you stay together... for better or worse... and you have to stay even if it's no good.

Then the marriage finally ends and they divorce and feel a failure and say, *It's difficult to cope after a divorce.* But does it have to be hard to cope after a divorce?

You weren't always in a relationship. You were an individual before you got married, right?

Many women are consumed to become a couple again. Not being attached is scary for some women. And some women are scared to get into a relationship because they're scared they are going to get hurt again. We need a balanced approach in all areas of life.

What is the worst thing if you got into a new relationship and it didn't work and you got hurt? What's the worst thing that's going to happen to you? So you feel hurt. So you have a broken heart.

Always know we get over it because we are more resilient then we realise. We can actually get over everything if we allow ourselves to process pain. You feel both joy and pain. It's all good emotions. That's how you build resilience by feeling it. It would be no different to a person who is going to become a marathon runner. To build resilience you need to push through all the pain barriers along the way and keep running.

What's the difference?

After divorce, its normal that you're trying to reset. I guess you're trying to find your identity as an individual again. And that's what you need to do. Remember, you started off as an individual.

Question yourself, *How do I need to come back to me to be okay with me?*

Many women go into a marriage because they didn't feel they had an identity. Getting married maybe completed their identity. But that's probably just conditioning. *You have to do this... and you have to get a good job... and you have to go to university... and you have to get married... and you have to buy a house...* but it's all conditioning.

And if you don't, then what would that mean?

But after a divorce you are an individual again, so you need to work out your most important values, wants and needs and then make conscious choices based on what's important to you. Take notice. *Where am I really within myself? What can I do on my own? How can I do I normally feel on my own?*

Importantly, you come to realise that you <u>are</u> able to cope. Ask yourself, *Where am I already being resilient? Where am I already capable? Self-reliant?*

Women ask me, *How do I build resilience?*

Well, you've actually already got it in you. So, it's just to question self. Where am I *already* capable and resilient? Where am I *already* coping?

Clinically, we talk about the perceived ability to cope (PAC). Look at what you can cope with *already*. That's how I had to think about it. Perceive that you *can* cope.

Where do I *already* have the ability to cope? Look within? That requires awareness.

Noticing that you need to notice instead of simply being triggered, reactive and in victim mode. Noticing any conditioning – should haves – that trigger that debilitating disparaging self- talk.

Achieving your success is also about acceptance. You need to accept that challenges are normal and that you can cope.

What I think happens to women when they've had heartbreak or they're hurting, or they are in a state of anger, or if their partner has had an affair, for example, they believe that they were not good enough.

And that's where the problem starts. You take something on that essentially is not your problem and become a victim.

Instead of saying, *That's not my problem. It's got nothing to do with me that my husband had an affair...* they start thinking, *I'm not good enough. I'm not pretty enough. I've got fat after I had my kid. I feel uncomfortable. He went off with another a younger woman.* That's what we've been saying all the time. They are trying to find a reason and typically start blaming themself.

Okay, as soon as you think, *I'm not good enough. I'm not pretty enough,* that's when you've lost your resilience. You've on-boarded the victim. You cannot have resilience if you're taking on the victim mentality. You cannot have resilience because who you're being is a problem in itself. Notice if you can't separate yourself from someone else's irresponsible behaviour.

It still hurts, but in most cases, women *sensed* or *knew* that their man was not on the same page value-wise. Women *know*... but they ignore their awareness.

Choose to accept that your highly capable of achieving anything you desire. Reinvest in your self-worth. Raise your value.

You're already future-pacing challenges. Listen to your inner guidance for advise. Appreciate your inner resilience that you will cope. Create the perceived ability to cope in your thinking... handle how you'll take on the challenges and accept success is coming your way.

Trust your awareness, always.

What resources have helped get me this far? That's looking backwards – resourcefully – rather than looking back looking for the cause of your current problems. Asking, *Who can I blame? What can I blame?* is looking backwards in a negative way.

Look backwards in a positive way. *OK, this happened, but what are the resources I've that got me through that? And could I probably use those same things going forward now?*

It's always about how we talk to ourselves. I look at the inner-resources I already have available. It might be hard and that's okay because I don't give up on myself anymore. If it is hard, I'm going to get through it because that's what I do.

I'm going to keep trying, keep moving forward. Keep being true to myself.

I also noticed that when I was dwelling in any negative self-talk I was in a paralysed state of inaction and saying to myself, *I can't cope...*or *poor me...* That thinking does not cultivate resilience. It's a block to any future success. If we just give up because we think we can't achieve, we are absolutely correct but the opposite is also true. Failure was never on my radar once I decided to succeed.

You never need to give up on your own success. You *can* do it. You are incredibly powerful.

What if you have constant challenges and constant feelings and emotions? So, what.

In my case, I *feel* them. I let pain go through me. I sit with it and question it and breath it out of my body. I breath out anything that does not serve me.

I want to feel that pain because I've learned that when I feel, I take on a positive action such as breathing it out and it helps cultivate the ability to cope under pressure. It's better than any self-sabotaging thoughts or behaviours and better than dwelling on the pain. *I know I'm going to come out the other end. There's no other way in my mind. And I want to feel all the goodness. I deserve to create my own happiness.*

It's good to be a human.

The more aware of what you are experiencing, the more learning and the more resilience you build. Appreciate yourself when things are going great and deal with things when they are not. Problems won't go away until you take action. Even little actions. Just deal with things as they come up.

And notice that you are *already* capable, you have the answers, and you have that inner resilience.

Your awareness of action creates your success. When your values are aligned with your actions you make you feel great enhancing your self-worth.

I am a higher performance coach, because... you can always take your performance higher.

About Sheron Kenny

Sheron Kenny is a business coach with qualifications in counselling. She started her professional career as a young successful salon owner which she credits for building up her resilience. She loves buying property and yoga and her morning walks on the beach.

Contact Sheron *linkedin.com/in/sheron-kenny-732a4a97*

Women Are Afraid to Own Their Greatness And It's Costing Them!

Alessandra Wall Ph.D

Whether navigating interviews for a new job or simply working on building your visibility in your current role, having the right words and framework to talk about what you bring to the table is beyond liberating, it's essential for anyone hoping to succeed at the highest levels of the proverbial ladder. Unfortunately, for most women this is surprisingly difficult to do.

Do me a small favor, grab a sheet of paper... Now answer this question: *How comfortable are you with sharing your value?* Think about it; now write down your answer (using a grade A-F) on your sheet of paper.

How Do You Compare?

What grade did you give yourself? The vast majority of women I speak with (65% or so) give themselves a solid C, a few fall in the B-zone (10%), many 20% give themselves failing grades (D - F), and the rest, a small portion of women, feel comfortable but are not always sure that they're going about it the right way.

Cocky Is A Bad Word (Double Standards Be Damned).

Why do most women feel very uncomfortable with sharing their value? Most women have been taught from the time they were in diapers to be humble, to use 'we' instead of 'me', to make others shine while they stand in their shadows, to keep their greatness to themselves.

So when someone like me tells women they need to clearly, confidently, and compellingly let others know what they bring to the table and the impact they can make with those skills, they squirm. This goes against everything they have been taught.

Interesting fact: I'm often told, 'In my culture girls and women are taught to be humble.' I've heard this from women raised in European and African countries, from American women as well as women from all over Asia and Latin America. This is a universal teaching social rule, it's not just you, it's all of us.

FACT - If you don't own plus share your value, then no one will know you belong at the top!

I know you don't want to hear this, but if you want a promotion, if you deserve that raise, if you're adamant that you WILL be hired by that company you love, to do a job that makes you feel like a million bucks, while earning a high six-figure salary, then you're going to have to promote yourself.

Bosses, clients, and teammates appreciate your contributions, but they've come to expect a stellar performance from you. No one is really keeping track of your work or your results.

Except for you... you know what it takes day in and day out to produce those results. You know what kind of impact you make for your team and your clients. You know what it takes to be this good, and so it's your responsibility to share that with every person who relies on your hard work to succeed.

Invisible Workhorse To Unforgettable Powerhouse; Get Seen And Promoted

My client Jess is brilliant, driven, hardworking, and good, very good at her job, but she's also self-effacing and struggled to share her value with others. Although her colleagues and supervisors loved her, she wasn't getting promoted to the leadership opportunities she wanted.

Jess was a powerhouse at work, but she lacked visibility and therefore recognition; so she wasn't accessing roles that would have been perfect for her.

We walked her through our *Recognition Systems*,

part of our *Impact & Influence* methodology, and taught her how to own, articulate, and comfortably share her skills and wins with others.

The result? In under six months, Jess had two exciting job offers, one created just for her by a former manager. She took that promotion and the 15% raise that came with it.

'I finally put an interview talk together, got asked to interview at two fantastic biotechs, and will be moving on to an exciting role literally made for me.'

It is your responsibility to educate others about your value and how you want your skill positioned.

It's Not Bragging...

Coaching isn't just about learning skills and holding people accountable. A big part of successfully coaching someone to the top is mindset transformation, which is where being a psychologist comes in very handy.

One of the biggest mindset shifts I help women make is owning their value without embarrassment or guilt, so they can effortlessly speak to their value without feeling uncomfortable or full of themselves.

Here's the secret: when you take the time to explain to others what you bring to the table, how you excel at it, and what you can do with that skill set, you are actually helping them. Articulating your value provides

ESSENTIAL information. Thanks to you, they'll finally understand exactly where to get the help and support they so desperately seek and need.

REPEAT AFTER ME --> *It's not bragging, it's educating.*

You're not full of yourself, you're speaking factually about the service you can provide. You're educating people, not making yourself feel good; there's a context to your sharing.

Another client, Amy, a Managing Director at a major financial institution, came to Noteworthy to build a strategic long-term plan for her career. Amy had dozens of opportunities to choose from; so many that it was impossible to yes to everything. What Amy wanted was to position herself for projects that were best aligned with her skillset and her needs. What Amy needed was for people to stop coming to her with every opportunity and instead seek her out for the once-in-a-lifetime opportunities that she deserved.

Here again, articulating her value with clarity and confidence was a major factor. Being known for the right things made it easier for her to say yes and no. She's established herself as an expert and is been sought after for promotions and new jobs without having to go look for them. Her most recent promotion landed her a 20% salary increase, a larger team, a bigger leadership network, and new responsibilities that will better position her for the C-suite.

You DON'T need to like talking about yourself.

You will have to learn how and where to do it well if you want to be seen, recognized, valued, hired, promoted, and paid very well for your skill.

Your Turn To Practice

Below are five different opportunities to talk about yourself, share your value, discuss your impact, and communicate your character without bragging or feeling like you're pitching yourself. Whether you're in the market for a new job, a promotion, or just trying to position yourself to do more of what you love and excel at, you now have a blueprint to build those opportunities.

Five Ways to Share Your Value To Elevate Your Brand And Your Impact

1. When Introducing Yourself To A New Team Or Client

It's great that your interviewers understand what you bring to the table, but the people who really need to understand your value are the members of your team. Whether it's in that first meeting when you're being introduced to your colleagues, or via more informal conversations in the first few weeks in your new position, take a few minutes to share with others what you do best, where you can add the most value, and who you are as a whole person.

2. When You Get Complimented

When most people get complimented the first thing they do is deflect the comment. 'Aw, thank you!' they say awkwardly. Or, 'It was nothing really!' There are a couple of reasons why this is a terrible way of receiving a compliment. First, it dismisses the effort the complimenter made in coming to you in the first place. Secondly, you are giving up a golden opportunity to help someone understand how you achieve excellence and how you can be positioned to repeat that achievement in the future. Instead, accept the compliment and use it as an opportunity to showcase your value.

Example: Casey, your supervisor, compliments you - the team leader - on the high quality of a recent deliverable.

You respond: Casey, I really appreciate you taking a minute to share that with me. Excellence is one of my core values, and I'm lucky enough to be good at reading and connecting with people and understanding what they bring to the table. That's how I knew that Reggie and Diana were perfect for this project and for the client.

If ever you need help with something like this in the future, don't hesitate to reach out, I love finding the perfect people for the job.'

3. When You Accept A Project Or Task

When you're asked to take on a task and you know you're perfect for the job, why not explain why you're excited to do the work and how your skillset will lend itself to a successful outcome?

4. When You Decline A Task

When declining a client or a project, talk about what is in your wheelhouse (what you love and excel at), and then explain that what's being asked of you isn't where you shine. Be ready with a list of alternate colleagues whom you believe are perfect for the job you just said no to. It's a win-win-win, you get to set boundaries, articulate your value, and elevate someone on your team, and the asker gets the help they need.

5. When You're Asked How You're Doing

You could say fine, or you could build visibility around your work and your skill, by very briefly explaining what you're working on and why it excites you.

Answering ubiquitous questions like 'how are you?' with real answers about what is and isn't working for you helps build relationships and trust and potentially gives someone a bit more context to understand you and what I bring to the table.

Even if you're not currently in the market for a new job visibility is essential if you're goal is to build a career that's both successful and fulfilling. Visibility is the most important factor associated with career growth and promotions for women; especially senior leaders. The best way to build visibility is to learn how to articulate your value in a manner that's both clear and compelling, so the people around understand both what you can do and care enough about you to feel invested in supporting your success.

About Alessandra Wall Ph.D

Dr. Alessandra Wall is the founder of Noteworthy, an executive coaching firm focused on elevating and empowering senior leading and executive women in STEM & finance. She has spent thousands of hours working with hundreds of women leaders the world over, helping them to be wildly successful and deeply fulfilled.

As a 15+ year clinical psychologist, she knows that degrees and experience, knowledge, and long hours aren't enough. She has earned the reputation of being a coach who combines strategic pragmatism, genuine empathy, and a deep understanding of the human mind to propel her clients further, faster, and better.

Dr. Wall wants to build a world where women at the highest levels of leadership and success are so common it's no longer noteworthy.

https://www.linkedin.com/in/dralessandrawall

www.noteworthyinc.co

Navigating Challenges

Katt Philipps

My life and career can be defined by the twists and turns it has taken. I started my post-collegiate career as a makeup artist in the film industry, where I would prep many a star for the stage. I loved the film industry's adventures until 17 years ago when I met my husband, and love brought me to a suburb of Chicago in 2006. Then, I dedicated my work to taking makeup off faces rather than applying it and began my career as a facialist.

I trained with physicians and in the spa for the next seven years. In 2013, when given the opportunity, I opened the doors of Gräfin, a small one-room clinic dedicated to facial treatments and wellness. In the beginning, things were slow, but by year two, I was performing back-to-back facials five days a week, and my business was growing rapidly. I had built a reputation as one of the best in the Midwest. My clients came from all over the world for their facials, often with their suitcases in tow. I was living my dream, and as my client list grew, I was thrilled about the many new business opportunities opening for me.

Enjoying the spoils of my success, my husband and I vacationed often. He and I were keen backpackers, kayakers, and all things outdoors. But on one of these trips, I woke up feeling very unwell, with a high fever, body aches, and great difficulty keeping thoughts in my head. At first, I thought it was just a cold or flu, but over the next ten days, my short-term memory loss became more and more problematic. Thankfully, the fever subsided as the days went on, but my cognitive symptoms did not. Being a stubborn woman, hoping I would get better, I did not seek medical assistance immediately, but as more and more signs popped up over the next year, I finally sought help. After countless appointments and puzzled physicians, we finally ran the proper test. After two years of decline, I was finally diagnosed with Lyme disease.

I was devastated. I had heard of Lyme disease before, but I never thought it could happen to me. I knew that the condition could have serious long-term effects, and in these two years, I struggled not to let it impact my career.

At first, I tried to keep up with my busy schedule. I pushed myself to keep going, despite the pain and exhaustion. But it soon became apparent that I needed to take a step back and focus on my health. I knew I had to cancel many of my appointments and take a break from work, but I couldn't imagine being away from my clients for even a week.

My body and mind were exhausted from my busy schedule, but not willing to give up on what I had built, I had to find another way.

As I tightened my work schedule from more than 45 hours a week down to 24, I worried about how my clients would react. I knew I would have to let many loyal in-person patrons go. To preserve the continuity of treatment for as many as possible, I began booking clients 12 months in advance. Many clients had been with me for years, and I knew they would be disappointed, but I had to choose myself and my health for the first time in my life.

The financial implications of the changes to my business were terrifying, but not as much as the hardship of turning my back on loyal facial guests. I started to think about what I could do to continue to serve my clients, even if I couldn't see them in person. I had a lot of knowledge and expertise to share and a desire to protect people from the shady side of skincare marketing. I knew then that I needed to take my business online.

I began to research online skincare stores, and I started to explore ways to bring the high-touch nature of the facial spa to the online space. I read as many books as possible on customer service and wrote notebooks full of ideas on bringing that service to an online store. At first, I was hesitant. I had never run an online business before and needed to learn about buying habits, marketing, fulfillment, SEO, and web design. There was a never-ending list of things to know and puzzles to solve. But as I delved deeper into online sales, I saw the potential. I realized I could reach a much wider audience than I ever could in person and help people all over the country.

At first, my online store was slow to gain traction. I had to work hard to build a customer base, and I spent long hours marketing skincare products through email and other channels. But over time, my business grew. My clients loved the products and the convenience of products directed to their door, and they began to share their experiences on social media, helping spread the word.

The clinic was running smoothly, my health was stable, and our online store was finally getting a solid following, and then the 2020 pandemic hit, forcing an eight-month shutdown of all in-person treatments. Up to this point, the lead financial driver for the business was in-person treatments, but the pandemic posed another issue. Suddenly, I couldn't get any products to sell. I had positioned myself as the place to purchase premier European skincare, but with several months of backlogs in the ports and customs at a near standstill, my shelves were bare. I made calls, but nothing was coming from my suppliers.

Searching everywhere for products, I discovered that a small supplier I had worked with was also sitting idle because of the shutdowns. With great caution and the advice of their team of experts, in May 2020, I began developing my skincare product line. I spent months researching and testing different ingredients, trying to create the perfect formulas for my clients. I worked closely with a graphic designer to create the packaging, hired photographers, and begged my husband to help me create a better website for my new online store.

As I worked on my new product line, I was surprised by how much I enjoyed the process. I loved being able to create something new and exciting, something that could help people feel better about themselves. Through skincare, I could touch faces from a distance and still positively change an individual's well-being. I poured my heart and soul into my new products and was thrilled when they started to take off.

Constant improvement of communication between myself and customers has been crucial to the success of my online store; I get my inspiration from the clients I still see in person. I thrive from personal connections, and their needs inspire not just the wording of the product descriptions but the direction of the product development. As I worked on my new business, I realized there were other ways to connect with people.

I started to offer online consultations, where I could talk to my clients face-to-face and offer them personalized advice and recommendations. I also started to share more of my personal story online, discussing my struggles with Lyme disease and how it impacted my life. By being more open and vulnerable, I could connect with my clients in new and meaningful ways.

As my business continued to grow, I started thinking

about how to use it to make a difference in the world. I began to explore opportunities for charitable partnerships, and I started to donate a portion of my profits to organizations working to do good in the world and help fight disease, homelessness, cruelty, and environmental causes. I also used my platform to raise awareness about the importance of self-care and overall health.

While I had never imagined that I would be forced to change my business model, I was grateful for the opportunities that it presented. Through my illness, I discovered new passions and ways of connecting with people. I learned that sometimes, the most significant challenges could be incredible growth opportunities.

Of course, there are still days when I struggle. Lyme disease is a chronic illness that can be challenging to manage. But I am no longer defined by my condition, and I have found new ways to channel my energy and passion.

Looking back on the past few years, I am proud of all I have accomplished. From starting my online store to raising charitable awareness for many worthy causes, I am making a difference in the world. And while my business may look different than it did before, I am grateful for the journey that brought me here.

I have learned that life can be unpredictable and that sometimes, we are forced to adapt to new circumstances. But no matter our challenges, we always have the power to make something beautiful out of them. And for me, that is the true beauty of life.

About Katt Philipps

After 30 years in the Industry, Spa Owner and Licensed Esthetician Katt Philipps has studied beauty from almost every angle. Katt's first career as a Hollywood makeup artist inspired her love of all things skin. Her curious nature and passion for people and education allowed her to  work in spas and medical offices before opening her bustling private skin clinic in the suburbs of Chicago. A passion for relationships and business strategy helped Katt build a multi-six-figure business as a solo esthetician.

Katt's busy beauty studio in the Chicago suburbs continues to be her inspiration as she shares what she has learned with others. With her husband Brian, Katt has continued to grow her business online using retail to bring awareness to different charities by donating a portion of every sale to a new charity every quarter. Katt

After being diagnosed with Lymes Disease in 2017, Katt has learned to simplify her work life by learning to be more strategic in business. She loves helping others 'uncomplicate' their businesses and has joyfully shared her story with multiple international beauty industry podcasts, speaking engagements, and a book.

Most days, you will find Katt enjoying nature on a

small family farm, tending bees, and enjoying a quiet life with her dogs and loving husband.

katt@grafinskin.com

www.grafinskin.com

instagram grafin_beauty

What If Slowing Down Is Really Speeding You Up?

Sammy Blindell

I sat at my desk, tears pouring down my face as heavy sobs convulsed throughout my entire body. It wasn't only my sobs that were making my body shake. Fear had gripped me so tightly that I was trying desperately to catch my breath between cries. 'I can't go through this again' I thought, as I could feel everything that I'd invested into myself, my team and the business over the past six years unravel before my very eyes.

Just one week before, I had flown back into the UK from a speaking tour across the East Coast of the States, where I had launched my business into Fort Lauderdale, Orlando, Atlanta, Savanna, and New York over the previous sixteen months. We had already grown into five cities around the UK, three cities in the Netherlands, Calgary, Singapore, Bali, and Brisbane, with Chicago, Nashville and eight other cities globally lined up to launch over the next nine months.

159

We were running 34 live in-person Mastermind events all around the world every month, plus members weekends, retreats, and strategy days. The plans for growth were exciting, yet underneath I was feeling incredibly guilty and sad about not being home enough for our children and fur-babies.

I had invested so much of myself into launching, growing, and expanding the business, that I was always on a plane or train traveling somewhere to speak, film, be interviewed, connect with our members, or to support my growing team as they launched into new cities around the world. Business was flying and, on the surface, so was I.

While all the travel and adventure looked glamorous across the surface of social media however, my schedule was grueling and left hardly any time for our at-home kids (17, 22 and 26 at the time), who were holding the fort while I traveled constantly, my husband joining me 95% of the time.

During the entire year of 2017, we had only been at home six weeks in total, which was made up of us flying in from wherever we'd been, throwing everything into the washing machine, taking the kids out to dinner to catch up, get back home, dry everything, pack it all, then maybe spend a day or two with them and the fur-babies before heading out for the airport again.

It was crazy.

Just four weeks before this ugly crying moment, Greg and I had moved into our dream home on the water. A sixty-one foot by twelve-foot barge, with the intention of 'slowing down a bit'. We had helped two of the kids move into their own homes and our youngest was excited to move down to London for university a few months later. Everything was flowing perfectly... until it wasn't.

As the announcement came on 23rd March 2020 that the world was now officially in lockdown, our business went into lockdown with it. I sat there, terrified like a rabbit in the headlights that I was about to lose it all again. I had already lost it all back in 2013 when I walked away from my multi-million pound branding agency, burned out and broken from being in business with what I now know to be a narcissist... delightful on the outside, but totally resentful, rotten, and rude to me whenever he got the chance behind closed doors. By the time I handed the keys of the business over on 30th September 2013, I'd been admitted to hospital four times with suspected heart attacks and was a crushed little shell of my old self. I was ready to hibernate.

I had already built another five businesses between 2002 – 2013 alongside the business with my partner, which meant I had a lot of business experience to draw on. So, when I felt well enough in early 2014, I launched my new business which started online initially. But as the physical memberships, events, retreats and speaking side of the business grew, it had become 90% of my incomings. Only 10% of revenue was coming from online business by March 2020 and I had been too busy traveling to realize how much I had let the online side of the business slip while focusing my attention on the events.

My husband and I had invested everything we had into growing the business and all our savings went on buying our dream home, so we had very little to fall back on. I had poured all my time into the events side of the business while it was growing, so I hadn't prepared myself at all for losing 90% of our income overnight.

While many of our members kept paying for a month or two as we turned 100% of our attention to supporting them online, they had joined our membership for the physical connections we were inviting them to each month. As soon as the physical meetups weren't possible anymore, online just wasn't enough. No matter how much support I poured into them online, the family and team I had invested six years of my life into building evaporated, along with my self-confidence, passion, and vision.

While I cried for my business, I also cried for all the time I felt I'd lost with our kids and families while pouring ourselves into the business so much.

I cried for all the years I had missed of my beloved dog's and cat's lives. I cried for all the money we'd lost, all the time we'd lost with each other and the time I had missed with my parents.

I cried in fear about what we would do next.

I cried for all the friendships with members that I'd built over the years who I wouldn't be seeing again now they had gone. All of this hit me hard, but what hit me hardest was not being able to leave the boat to see our kids now that we were finally home for the first time in six years.

It was a shock to be home so much at first. But as the shock wore off, the relief of not being allowed to go anywhere was palpable as the pressure of always needing to be in a million places at once drained from our nervous systems.

I did what I know best in moments of fight, flight, or freeze, and that is to serve.

For the next eight months that meant showing up every day to deliver training and masterminding for all the members that stayed, and welcome new members on board who were joining the new model of mastermind membership I created. If my members didn't have a business then I didn't have a business, so I set to work on doing everything I could do to help them get visible, go viral, and grow globally.

I launched books with my members, bought friends in from The Secret to train them, launched a daily show to interview them and ran monthly summits to give them a platform to spread their voices to the world. I started a monthly movie night and launched free programs for my community to help them get back on their feet financially. I even launched my own global movement, along with a charitable initiative that bought hundreds of the top speakers, trainers, and coaches I'd had the pleasure of sharing large stages with over the years to mastermind with my tribe as we raised thousands for charity each month.

The membership started to grow again as lots of new and growing businesses started going through the new programs and online courses. I put myself at the center of all their business problems, listening to their needs and creating solutions on demand, supporting them in every way I could. We celebrated hundreds of business growth successes throughout lockdown, and many global movements were born as we supported our members to brand, build and expand the online sides of their businesses. From the depths of despair, we grew our roots. Then, we grew our wings.

Did I feel like giving up lots of times? Yes

Did I want to hibernate when fear showed its ugly head? *Absofrickinglutely!*

Did I sometimes lose sight of my vision? Of course.

But I always had a saying rolling around in my head whenever it got tough…

'I'm doing the things today that other people won't, so I can do the things in future that other people can't.'

I am now living a life that other people can't because I did the things that others wouldn't do. I did what needed to be done, put in the crazy hours when I had to, and put my clients at the heart of everything instead of my ego. Ahh yes, my ego. I learned a lot about my ego during this time, but I will have to save that for another book!

Now online sales make up 100% of our revenue and we get to see our kids and families whenever we like. Our time is spent going on lot of adventures in the Land Rover that we converted to stealth camp all over the country. Our fur-babies come with us and enjoy the adventures as much as we do! Work can happen from wherever we are, so we no longer must be in a geographical location to earn money. Apart from several speaking opportunities that I say yes to per year, it's now very rare for us to go away for work and the beauty is that we no longer need to leave home to go to work.

To say all this success came with massive highs and incredible lows would be an understatement! But looking back on it all now, it was totally worth the experience just to be able to support so many other women in business who are now starting out where I started. I've learned so much and still thoroughly enjoy masterminding with my members every day and delivering our monthly programs. I love getting to see their growth and be part of it right from the very heart of it. I could never have done this while flying all over the place.

My greatest learning throughout all of this is that prior to this experience, I invested a lot of time, money, and energy driving people to my business from the outside in. But it was only when I couldn't do it anymore that I started serving from the inside out, pouring myself into supporting, nurturing, and valuing those who were already in my communities. What I hadn't expected was that all that attention focused on them meant that I no longer had to do any marketing at all, because they were going out and doing it all for me through referrals.

I also didn't realize how much intellectual property I was creating by being responsive to my members. Building everything around them means that I have now created over 1,000 online courses, resources, programs, downloads, templates, worksheets, cheat sheets, and books, not including the hundreds of articles I have written to help them thrive. I now have a global online resource that supports small business owners to take control of their own brand and a brilliant brand visibility program that I launched with my husband at the beginning of 2023 to support entrepreneurs to be fearlessly visible.

Yes, part of me still craves the physical, live-in-person model. However, the rest of me loves being at home too much now to pull myself into a million pieces again.

If I can give you one thing, it is to remind you that everything, and I mean EVERYTHING, is always happening FOR you for a reason. It is happening for you, so that at some point in your life when it feels right, it can move THROUGH you or through your business to others.

And maybe one day it will even be guided BY you, and you will create a movement that creates a ripple effect in the lives of many people.

I will leave you with something I wrote for my new book in the hope that it inspires you to put your big girl panties on and go for it...

You are too precious to stay hidden.

You are too gifted to stay scared.

You are too needed to stay silent.

You are too big to play small.

It's now time for you to fearlessly, relentlessly, courageously, and unapologetically go out there and make the juicy ripples of impact that you, and only you, were born to make.

I am wishing you the whole universe of love, blessings and prosperity on this next step of your journey and always remember... You've got this!

About Sammy Blindell
The Brand Builder Global Ripple Maker
& Brand Visibility Mentor

Sammy is a multi-award-winning international speaker, eight times best-selling author, How To Build A Brand Global CEO, and Founder of One Drop Movement.

After 13 years in branding, followed by 11 years building her first five businesses, Sammy burned out, handing over her £7.8m company in 2013 to rebuild her health. By 2014, her business passion returned, along with a quest to do what she loves online; reaching more people in less time, with less stress, more time freedom, AND making good money to do good with.

Her vision to build the world's most practical online brand building resource for entrepreneurs was born, along with her first program, making $23,000 a month in the first 12 weeks. After launching a further 1000+ online courses and resources, she developed an easy-to-follow brand building cashflow system for others to do it too. Over 65,000+ entrepreneurs have followed it. Could you be next?

Website: *www.OneDropMovement.com*

Email: *Sammy@OneDropMovement.com*

LinkedIn: *www.linkedin.com/in/sammyblindell*

Facebook: *www.facebook.com/groups/ onedropmovementglobal*

Instagram: *www.instagram.com/onedropmovement*

Three Ways Business Women Can Become More Resilient

Elena Meskhi

Resilience. Do I have such a quality, and how appropriate is it for me to write on this topic? That's what I thought initially when I got the request. And then, while I was brewing over the whole concept, I realized my potential. Just how resilient could I be? And how have I developed my resilience?

As an accountant and a tax advisor in the United Kingdom, running the accountancy practice and leading a team of professionals, I always feel like being on the front line. If I do not solve my crisis, then I have many cases from the clients to solve. Have you ever heard of the tax investigation? Well, we handle that too. My husband calls me a crisis manager, and I'm starting to see why.

In fewer than 48 hours, one of my biggest clients collapsed and took the decision to file for bankruptcy, and one of the key players in my team filed for resignation with immediate effect. These are totally unconnected events, with the only connection being myself and my business. But each requires resilience under pressure. Resilience, you say?

My journey started 18 years ago. I have gone through up and downs in the professional industry and still going through it. On the way, I got married, had three kids, founded a few businesses, sold my practice, started again and rebuilt from scratch. In the course of my professional career, I have helped thousands of clients, mainly business owners, big and small. Now, I mainly work with very successful business owners. Over time, I have identified how they stay resilient.

They take care of their body, trust their intuition, and have interests outside of their business. I want to elaborate on each of those qualities, which are important, especially if you are a business woman.

Appreciate Your Body And Take Care Of It

Everybody emphasizes the importance of a healthy body, and taking care of your health, so I know this advice does not win the prize for Mrs Genius. However, I really want to share it with you from a different angle.

Your body is capable of functioning between 100 and 120 years. Your body is not designed to experience any devastating health problems but we make it sick with our own actions or inactions. We take our health for granted, we don't take good care of or we simply abuse or neglect our bodies.

Well, at least I had the first 25 years and came to my senses then. Fortunately, 25 years have not done that much damage to my body, which I could not reverse. I was testing my body limits since birth; falling and breaking my legs, climbing fences, fighting (like any child would), over-exercising, overeating, and overdrinking in my teenage years. I have done all sorts of 'tests' with my body we do on a daily basis. When I say take care of our body, I mean not only physical elements of it like eating healthy food, drinking lots of water and physically exercising but keeping it in an emotional comfort state too.

I call it keeping your body in a *pure state*.

The pure state of the body is when all physical comfort conditions are met: hunger and thirst satisfied, body exercised and relaxed. *Relaxed* is a keyword. Yes, we can experience moments of bursts of adrenaline and cortisol here and there, but we know the methods of how to release it. We use professional help to release it; we do not live in high gear all the time. We can harm our bodies in many different ways: suppressing anger, not exercising or exercising too much, and exhausting our bodies with poor diets or too much food.

And then there are psychosomatic conditions (a physical illness or other condition) caused or aggravated by a mental factor such as internal conflict or stress. This is when our body becomes ill, for example, due to excessive thoughts, feelings or concerns about symptoms — which affects the ability to function well. Or when we suppress emotions in our body.

That's why it's important to get to know your body and to learn how to release and express emotions.

It is said that all illnesses start from the head. Mental and physical health are very closely linked. When we overeat, there is a likelihood that we are trying to compensate for some of our insecurities.

Comfort eating is driven by the motivation to shut down uncomfortable feelings. The Hollywood cliche, when you are upset, is to reach for a bucket of ice cream, tissues and a sad movie as a way of coping with the dramas and disappointments of life.

But go deeper than that remedy; work with your feelings, and balance your body and mind.

Keeping your body in a pure state means maintaining it in harmony with your mind, physical health and mental health.

I recommend that you build a team of professionals you can refer to should you have a need: dentists, osteopaths, therapists, counsellors, physiotherapists, psychotherapists, homoeopaths, and all other medical body-related professionals you have access to.

Make it a personal goal to have harmony in your body and mind and start with the most important aspect of your body right now. Better yet, make it a personal hobby.

Trust Your Intuition

The more control we have over our health the easier it becomes to hear what the body says. Especially us women. If I may refer back to the source here:

God "formed man of the dust of the ground, and breathed into his nostrils the breath of life, and man became a living soul" (Genesis 2:7).

God recognized this and caused Adam to fall into a deep sleep. He then took one of Adam's ribs from him, which he fashioned into a woman, who was called Eve.
(Genesis 2:21-22)

You have noticed the difference, right? We, women, have been created from the human flesh to start with. You might say we are *meant* to get connected with our bodies.

Let's fast forward from that moment and identify ourselves today. We have fought for our rights, the right to vote, the right to express our opinions, and the right to take management positions, hard and viciously, myself included.

We fought with men as if we were trying to become one. Yay! And what do we have now?

We are the winners; we got our rights back. We work like men, we party like men, but we also keep doing the part that women were doing all long. We run the companies, sit and lead at the boarding room, close the deals, we take executive decisions... just so we can finish early and rush to pick up kids from school and then cook dinner and then tidy up. Did I forget something? Oh, yes, feel grumpy about our men and partners who do not do the house chores. Why would we, since we fought so hard for our rights?

In all that fight for independence, we got distracted and carried away in this desire to become a man. Got carried away so far that we forgot about our natural powers, magnetism, intuition, and persuasion. And woman's resilience.

A woman leader is a natural woman state. Resilience comes naturally to us. We are meant to raise kids/ employees, build and nourish family/company, and guide and advise husbands/managers on what needs to be done to prosper and move forward. Resilience is a total woman's quality, the eagerness to succeed and perseverance in any challenging situations

Only when our body is taken care of, can we rely on our intuition, and our gut instincts. When our body is a mess, it is tough to identify any impulses at all: how would you distinguish whether it is gut instinct or gas?

Intuition comes in different forms: Someone gets it from the gut, someone gets it in a dream, someone gets it as a sort of inner voice providing advice. We all have different ways of receiving nudges from our intuition.

If you are ready to develop your intuition, I would suggest starting to get to pay close attention to how it shows up for you... most. As we say in NLP (neuro-linguistic programming): *calibrate it.*

But start small.

Imagine you are about to meet a new person (new client, prospect, candidate). You've spoken on the phone, but you have not met in person yet. How do you think he/she would look or dress or present, how old, what colour hair they got? And then cross-check, research, and meet the person? How far or close were you?

Ordering food in the restaurant: go for a new dish. Do you think it would be too salty, or just fine, hot or warm, would you like it or not? I would recommend you practice by going for qualities you will not be able to guess.

The goal is to notice how your intuition gets your attention. Trust your gut and then cross-check your responses. At some point, you will achieve the state when you know exactly how the intuitive signal is coming to you and what it means for you.

That's why calibration is important.

Let me share a story about one of my clients.

My client has been running the company for nine years, and she feels that no matter what she does, she keeps making the wrong choices. Bad management? She was convinced that her intuition was letting her down. Out of all candidates for the manager position, she choose the one who would later steal from her company! Out of all possible stock quotes, she picked up the company that then went bankrupt! Her company performed better when she was on holiday! Her manager did a better job than under her control! The list was endless.

After a few meetings, it became apparent to me that her intuition was not failing her at all. Her intuition was spot on. Intuitively, she knew she did not want to run that company anymore. She wanted to get rid of it and do something else. But she wasn't tuned in. Her calibration was wrong. When she realized this, she tuned into how her intuition shows up, and she set up a positive new plan to build and polish the company and sell it. She stopped sabotaging herself.

Have An Interest Outside Of Your Business

And the third final point, which I came across through trial and error, I found to be soul healing. What generates your creativity and helps you keep going, no matter what, is having other interests outside of your business.

Those interests should not be kids, family, partner or your house. It should be the different type of activity you do where you dive into and forget about everything. It sounds like you are doing your favourite work or cleaning the house.

Let's eliminate those examples of activity first.

Cleaning the house, ironing, and even cooking every day is not going to work here. Although all of the above are splendid activities to lose yourself and switch from work, it is not what we are looking for.

Remember the gender revolution I have mentioned above? That's one of the reasons why. Deep down, women leaders hate those chores because it's undermining our talents. And most of us delegate it to housekeepers anyway.

The activity should be something that you enjoy so much, that you completely lose yourself. That could be the piano, the plant you plant, or growing a specific type of flower, drawing, pottery, singing, dancing, writing, learning a new language, or learning any new skill.

The main criterion is that you should love it.

This trick might work: *remember yourself when you were 16-18 years old.* Did you have any sort of activity from the above list or outside of it that absorbed you totally? That might be it.

Again, please do not confuse about exercising. Don't try, cheat yourself and make two points with one activity like looking after your body, and having interest outside of work. It can work for the short term until exercising become your habit, and then it will stop working. That's not the trick we're looking for.

You really need to find the type of activity which really going to enhance and stimulate your creativity where you would be able to connect with the source of energy.

What will that help you achieve?

First of all, when you get out of your business you will have the opportunity to see things differently; and different things. Remember the old saying: 'I can't see the forest for the trees?' This is very much what happens when the business owner works 24/7. We are talking about continuously doing the same type of activity, making you a bad professional, a bad specialist in the area you do because you don't have the opportunity to withdraw yourself from that activity and then refresh your site and come back with a fresh look at the case, situation, the team, the workflow, the processes, whatever you ever see or run.

Doing things in entirely different industries or types of activity will help your brain switch into a different gear, and give the professional part of your brain oxygen to calibrate.

Activity outside of work boosts your creativity.

Clients who took this advice reported that they got many insights and revelations, exactly during the periods when they were immersed in their hobby.

And third, it will make you, at the very least, a nicer person because, believe me, it's very boring to talk to a person who only talks about business and their business challenges. If the person has any other interests which are as enjoyable for that person as his own business, that is a much more interesting opponent in conversation. Having interests outside of work adds a positive and creative dimension to your life.

If I had the opportunity to give advice to my young self 18 years ago when all this had just started, I would advise precisely that. I'm sure that by using those techniques, I would have fewer wrinkles, at least.

About Elena Meskhi

Elena Meskhi is a certified accountant, and tax advisor who leads a team of accountants and tax advisors in the firm Elena Meskhi & Co. Elena is also a non-executive director on the board of several companies, where she contributes her expertise and experience in running a business.

Elena@elenameskhi.com

elenameskhi.com

LIFE Skills For Success

Susan Routledge

For over 30 years I have had the absolute pleasure of employing female teams in my numerous businesses. I also have the pleasure to work as an International Business Consultant and to mentor so many fantastic beauty business owners within Beauty Directors Club.

I have witnessed firsthand, the incredible power of resilience in the lives of women. I have seen women overcome seemingly insurmountable obstacles and coming out stronger, more confident and with greater increased success.

My love is helping others to *Reach for The Stars*, and it makes me so proud when they achieve their greatest goals and realizing their true potential.

All I can ever remember wanting, was to be in the beauty industry. As a child, I loved the thought enhancing someone's looks with my hand-me- down cosmetics collection, much to the horror of any visitors (victims!!) who came to my home, and then dared to linger for any length of time.

I was really timid as a child, but I was brought up by the perfect parents, for me.

My Mother, the perfect homemaker who truly believed I could be and do anything. And my Father, a hard-working Foreman Joiner by day, and a Property Developer Entrepreneur by night, and every weekend.

But I wanted to get into the beauty industry.

My Dad's strategy was to work like crazy, make as many property investments as possible and then to retire early at 55, and live off the profits. So, the fact that I wanted to go to college to study Beauty Therapy and Hairdressing, which back in the late 1970s was a four-year course, seemed totally crazy to him.

The nearest courses were hundreds of miles away… but then, a course opened up in my region and I enrolled despite increasing pressure from my Dad to find a job.

When I graduated I discovered any decent jobs were miles away, but without telling my Dad, I decided to start a beauty and hairdressing freelancing business.

So, with flyers in hand, my Mum and I spent a full day posting leaflets out. To my total surprise, the hallway telephone was ringing by the time we got back.

So, I started the next day, with my car packed and ready to visit my first clients and with my Mum at home as my makeshift receptionist.

And I became so busy... *so quickly.*

There were only two things wrong; about 95% of my clients wanted hairdressing services not yet available in my small country town. Soon I was working ridiculous hours as I didn't want to let anyone down, or to turn anyone away.

I was succeeding but still hadn't told my Dad and I decided to keep my success under wraps until I could unequivocally prove my achievements to him. I had this vision of showing him my amazing accounts book and my Dad being so, so proud.

That day never came.

On an early February night, my Dad went to bed and never woke up again. He was only 50. He had a huge cerebral haemorrhage which instantly ended his life.

It just didn't seem real. I just couldn't take it in.

I had driven passed my Dad the day before. He was up a ladder and looked busy and I certainly didn't have time to stop as I was racing to my next appointment. I just thought I would see him later, but that was never to be. I didn't know what to do. I wanted to just run away, but I had all of my clients to see. Cancelling them just meant a longer wait list, so I did what I thought my

Dad would expect me to do and carried on working as much as I could.

I started to resent the business I had created, I resented that it was so demanding, that I had no free time, that it had stopped me chatting to my Dad on that last day of his life. I resented that I hadn't had chance to show him my accounts book, I resented everything, including that it wasn't even the career that I wanted. I realized that I just wanted to prove to my Dad I could do it, and now I was trapped in it all.

I now firmly believe that the universe will always correct things, and although no-one could bring my Dad back, I believe that there are external forces helping us.

Within weeks of my Dad's death, I developed a really severe rash over all of my hands. I had always protected my hands with gloves whilst working, but this rash came out of the blue and I started reacting to everything associated with hair products.

It was so painful that it would make me cry. I was so low anyway, but just putting this happy face on for the world.

My GP told me that I must look for another career. It was a relief, but I also had so many clients and responsibilities, but I knew I couldn't go on. But by now this business had no meaning to me and I literally just gave my whole business away to another local stylist.

Over the next couple of years, I took on retail jobs. I just wanted minimum responsibility and time to heal. I stumbled upon a book by Louise Hay called, *'You Can Heal Your Life'*. I was fascinated, and this started my never-ending journey in self-development.

By now the Beauty Industry was gaining momentum and I decided to take some refresher courses and start all over again.

I now had a clear vision and total belief that I was on the right path for ME, and nothing was going to stop me. I started freelancing again, but this time just in beauty therapy, and also got a position teaching in a private college one day a week.

Within exactly one year, I opened my first small salon. I then purchased premises, and with gradual expansion, we became the largest Beauty Salon in my region and one of the largest in the UK.

I wrote myself a note declaring that my salon would win the title of *'Professional Beauty Best Large UK Beauty Salon'*. It was a really big ask as previous winners all seemed to be well known city center salons and my business was unknown and 14 miles from any city.

We proudly won the title in 2007.

This was the start of winning over twelve National Business Awards and many other business accolades.

I have always created amazing teams around me, and I systematized the business to work independently of me.

This worked perfectly as it gave my team a chance to develop further. I always support my team to follow their dreams and keep in touch with most who are now spread as far as Australia. I am so proud that for a period of over 25 years, we never lost a therapist to another salon.

We have a constant staff training and development program, which freed my time to avidly travel to develop advanced business skills from some of the world's top entrepreneurs.

I was being constantly asked for advice from other salon owners on how they could successfully grow their salon and win national awards too.

Amongst giving so much free advice, I also became fascinated with how two salons could look totally the same on the surface, yet one would be flourishing, whilst the other was failing.

I invested heavily in a totally unique program working closely for a year with a global business turnaround expert and a small team of five other entrepreneurs, learning first-hand skills, transforming the fortunes of distressed businesses. What I learnt was invaluable. I perfected a business formula that would transform a salon business of any size or condition and trademarked my formula.

From here onwards, I have had the great pleasure of still owning my salon, with a fantastic team and wonderful clients, many who have been with us over 30 years.

I also have the pleasure to work as an International Business Consultant and work on a daily basis with so many fantastic beauty business owners within Beauty Directors Club.

I am blessed to attract the best clients and the most amazing network of people to work with.

My love is helping others to *Reach for The Stars* too and it makes me so proud when they achieve their greatest goals.

Along my business journey, I realized that to achieve continued consistent success. I needed a robust structure that I could call upon every day to keep me on track. From this need, I created my own personal formula to *Reach for The Stars* using the acronym of L I F E.

L I F E is simply looking at four elements of your life to focus on every day, to help to cultivate the skills and mindset needed to achieve success in both life and business. It consists of LOVE, INVEST, FOCUS, EXPECT.

LOVE

The first pillar of resilience is Love.

I always aim to only do what I love. I send love to myself daily. I also ensure I see the best in everything and send love to everyone and absolutely everything.

In return, I only attract the best people to me and amazing opportunities. Without fail, self-love is critical for women to succeed in business and in life.

As a mentor, I encourage women to prioritize self-care, set boundaries and to take control of their own well-being. I believe that self-love and self- care is a non-negotiable and makes you better equipped to tackle challenges and achieve goals.

I encourage everyone to set aside some time for themselves each day. This could mean going for a short walk, reading a book, meditating, or simply taking a few deep breaths. It is important for women to prioritize their mental and emotional health as well as their physical wellbeing.

Another way to practice self-love is by setting boundaries. There is so much pressure to do it all - to be the perfect boss, employee, parent, partner, friend, daughter but the reality is that we must set limits. Sometimes we just need to say NO or at the least delegate some tasks.

It is so important to recognize limits and to set boundaries to protect your time and energy.

Thinking time is often the most important time so make sure you have some time to concentrate on gratitude and day-dreaming your future into reality.

INVEST

The second pillar of resilience is Invest.

I invest time and energy in myself daily. Meditation is a non- negotiable investment of my time as part of my morning routine. We all have 1440 minutes in a day, and it is crucial to make sure you invest your time wisely. My other non-negotiable elements of my time are spending time in nature, journaling, and visualizing what I want to create. I have a never-ending thirst for personal development and business development, so I spend time learning every day via podcasts, books, and video content.

Women who invest in themselves and their careers are more likely to achieve success. I always encourage women to seek out mentors, learn from peers, attend workshops and conferences and to join industry associations. It is always beneficial to look at your time management. Often time can be totally wasted on menial tasks that someone else could do. Make managing your time your number one investment in yourself.

We live in a fast paced ever changing world so to stay resilient you must be continually investing in maximizing your time and knowledge.

FOCUS

The third pillar of resilience is Focus.

I only focus forwards and in a positive way. You can only use the past as feedback to drive your future to a new level. Dwelling in the past has no benefits at all. I believe that everything happens for a reason and is a way to give us emotional feedback and an opportunity to think better thoughts and to make better decisions in the future. I don't ever dwell in negativity as it keeps you stuck and attracts more of the same.

Women who are focused forwards on their goals are better equipped to overcome obstacles and to stay on track. This means setting clear detailed goals, creating action plans and vision, and holding themselves accountable. This is where the power of a mastermind or working with other like-minded women becomes price-less. Staying accountable keeps you forward thinking and then great ideas will multiply.

As a mentor, I encourage women to break down their goals into smaller achievable steps and to celebrate their success along the way. It is important to use any setbacks and challenges as essential feedback and to stay focused on the bigger goal which sometimes must have some twists and turns to lead you on the road to success.

I am a huge believer in the Laws of Attraction and staying positive is essential. Listen to the self-talk and stories that you are telling yourself and be very aware if you are focusing on problems or solutions. You can never solve a problem by focusing on the negative side. You must focus on the solution and the answers will come or the problem will naturally subside.

EXPECT

The fourth and final pillar of resilience is Expect.

This is a huge one. You can only create what you truly believe. I believe that I can create anything that anyone else has achieved, and you can too. Women who expect success are more likely to achieve it. This means maintaining a positive mindset, believing in themselves, and being willing to take risks.

I now use L I F E as a formula to help others to stay strong and resilient in any circumstances. The four pillars I use, never fail to build success.

I believe that I can create anything that anyone else has achieved, and you can too. My true wish for you, is to live a fantastic life created by yourself, for yourself.

Do L I F E and... *Reach for The Stars!!*

About Susan Routledge

Susan Routledge is a Multi Award Winning Salon Owner, International Business Consultant and trusted Industry Advisor. Susan has been in the Beauty Industry for over 35 years and is recognized in the Top UK Industry Influencers for her passion and dedication. She is also part of the  Professional Board for BABTAC helping to represent and raise Industry Standards for the Beauty Industry

Susan is the founder of her trademarked STABLE business formula, plus the Author of 'The Little Book of Client Retention' and Best Seller Co-Author of 'Your Best Life'.

Her down to earth, light-hearted approach has made her an International Speaker and an established Awards Judge.

She has an online business turnaround program called 'Salon Success Freedom' and is the creator of Beauty Directors Club, an ever-growing global membership and close community for salon, clinic and spa business owners with resources and multi expert advice.

Susan's online blog, Beauty Entrepreneurs, has attracted over 7,000 global subscribers for her weekly hints, tips and insights.

http://susanroutledge.com

http://beautydirectorsclub.com

https://www.facebook.com/groups/beautyentrepreneurshub

Podcasting Gave Me a Voice: How Sharing My Story Became A Platform for Empowerment

Kim Hayden

One of the most important lessons I have ever learned in my life happened in fourth grade. I would walk to my grandparents after school. I loved going to my grandparents' home. Not only was I guaranteed a snack and a great visit, but I also had friends on the block. My friends Teri and Kathy had fun chatting after school. Kathy's grandmother lived across the street from my grandparents and just three homes from Teri's little red house. At Kathy's grandma's house we were lucky to get a bottle of Coke and snacks.

Spring of my fourth grade year the three of us converged for the after school gabfest with our coveted soda pop. Kathy started to share all the drama that went down in her school that day. The police had come to talk with a classmate. This wasn't like when the police come and give a chat about why the police are good or how you can be a good citizen. This was a visit to a specific little girl. You see, it was reported that her grandfather was abusing her. The police were there to take a statement and look into further actions.

My world stopped. I couldn't breathe, I couldn't hear anything, my body went hot, yet my fingers were ice cold. The Coke that I was enjoying just a moment before, threatened to revisit my mouth and not in a good way. This was wrong? This was wrong! I always knew things were not right with my father. Our secret was a secret for a reason. Because it was wrong.

I was devastated by this news because I too knew what it was like to live with abuse. For me, this was a turning point. It was the first time I realized that speaking up could make a difference, even if it meant risking being dismissed or disbelieved.

As I went across the street and told my grandmother what had happened, I remember feeling like my voice had finally been heard. Someone was listening, and that made all the difference. Unfortunately, when my mom was told about what happened, she didn't believe me. Because of my history of ADHD and trauma, I was often accused of exaggerating or lying, so no one took me seriously. The Catholic Counseling services were called, and after a few short months, everything was dismissed as an exaggeration.

For the next five years, I was silent. I didn't speak up about the abuse happening in my home.

But eventually, in ninth grade, I was heard and believed. It was a turning point for me because it showed me that every voice matters. That the pretext is to help understand, not to dismiss. That I am not alone and my voice matters. This lesson has literally shaped who I am today and the quest I am on.

I do want to point out at this time, I was gifted an amazing hero, Barbara Williams. Barb chose to be the voice for those who were dismissed, those who were ignored and those who lacked the strength to speak up. Barb was the silver lining in the storm of my life. That even though I had attempted suicide just to get anyone to listen, Barb stepped in to be my advocate. She would speak up in the courts, to my mother and even went toe to toe with my father. Barb taught me that my voice matters. That I matter. I also learned the power of advocacy and mentorship.

Fast forward four decades, and I have had a pretty awesome life. I have three kids, a happy marriage,and a career that has allowed me to serve my community and support the people within. I have been recognized with numerous industry awards and civic recognition as a visible community leader. As a community-minded entrepreneur, I have always searched for the next opportunity to serve. Food drives, community events, and volunteering where needed have all been part of my success.

However, there was always something missing. Despite all my successes, I still felt like my voice was not being heard. I felt like I was speaking, but no one was really listening. It wasn't until I discovered podcasting that I finally felt like I had a platform to truly share my voice.

Podcasting gave me a voice in a way that I never thought was possible. It allowed me to share my story and connect with others who had similar experiences. Through my podcast, I was able to reach a wider audience and share my message of hope and healing with others. It was a platform that allowed me to speak my truth and be heard.

The power of podcasting lies in its ability to connect people from all walks of life. It is a medium that allows for storytelling and conversation, and it is incredibly accessible. Anyone can start a podcast with just a microphone and an idea. For me, podcasting has been a lifeline. It has given me the opportunity to connect with others, share my story, and create a community of like-minded individuals who support one another.

Through podcasting, I have been able to share my experiences with amazing women from around the world. My experiences of building a successful business, of raising my children and of my formative years spent in trauma and abuse. Finding a strength within the sharing of my story and knowing I am not alone.

One of the most important things that podcasting has taught me is that every voice matters. It doesn't matter if you are a survivor of abuse, a mental health expert, or someone with an important story to tell.

All you need is one person to listen in, to feel valued, heard and supported. One person is like a single stone in a pond, that one person creates ripples and those ripples can multiply and mold the environment around the pond.

Through my podcast, I have been able to connect with people from all walks of life. I have interviewed survivors of abuse, mental health professionals, community activists, entrepreneurs, leaders and thought leaders.

I have shared stories of hope and resilience, and have explored the many different paths to healing. The feedback that I have received has been overwhelming, with many listeners telling me that my podcast has helped them to feel less alone, and to find the courage to speak up about their own experiences. I am always deeply grateful when a guest says it was an incredible experience for them.

This is what I call a win-win-win scenario.

'Kim Hayden is a force of greatness, leading the charge as an independent, strong, businesswoman who is always looking for ways to reach out and help others along the way. I am honored to call her my friend and I am continually inspired and in awe of her energy and communication skills. Keep changing the world for the better Kim! You are on a roll!' Debbie B

Podcasting has given me the power to amplify voices that might otherwise go unheard. It has allowed me to shine a light on the many issues that are important to me, and to create a platform for change. I have used my podcast to raise awareness about the importance of mental health, the impact of trauma on our lives, the need for community support, the struggles of building a business and of course the ever elusive work/life balance myth or magic.

I have also used my podcast as a tool to connect with other community leaders, and to collaborate on projects that benefit our shared community. Through podcasting, we can share our experiences, our struggles, and our triumphs, and create a community that is based on empathy and understanding.

If you are thinking about starting a podcast, I encourage you to take the leap. I am here to support you, either in the literal sense with one of my programs around podcasting, or even as a guest on my show. It can be intimidating to put your voice out there, but the rewards are immeasurable.

You will have the opportunity to connect with people from all over the world, to share your story, and to create a platform that can serve those you want to elevate.

In today's world there is no reason to sit quietly and hope someone comes to save you. You can be the hero of your story and you just may end up being a hero for someone else.

Stories are the currency of a rich mind. Share yours, speak up. We all learn through story. Whether on a podcast, speaking for a community initiative, writing an article for a magazine or even joining in a multi-author book like this one. The opportunities to be heard are limitless today!

I look forward to hearing your story!

About Kim Hayden

From Kansas to Canada, Kim has always worked to be a good neighbor and leader. In every endeavor through Servant Leadership, Kim has repeatedly excelled in several industries. A 22 year award winning Real Estate Career , TV Producer, Red Carpet, Event Host , Author and  Producer are just a few of Kim's accomplishments. Now bringing a lifetime of experiences and work together in the form of the Resilient Series, Kim is on a quest to grow audience awareness and expand the stage by working with women to create their multimedia authority content and produce opportunities through agency.

Self proclaimed Queen of Resilience, Kim Hayden addresses the pain points of Confidence, Credibility and Relevance that many women are challenged with, by sharing Kim's stories and strategies that built a six and seven figure career while overcoming the 'imposter' feel due to a childhood of disadvantage.

Founder of Resilient New Media and the Resilient Series, Kim works to provide opportunities through live/virtual events, Multi-Author books, the Resilient Women Magazine, Kim Talks Resilience Podcast and Podcasting workshops and guesting etiquette and agency.

Listen and Lean into our Resilient Community! Get your free monthly magazine and community network. *www.resilientgift.com* Did I mention.... totally FREE!

Podcast: *https://podcasts.apple.com/us/podcast/kim-talks-resilience/id1563051828*

Instagram: *https://www.instagram.com/resilientseries/*

Facebook: *https://www.facebook.com/KimTalksca*

YouTube: *https://www.youtube.com/channel/UCowz4fs2_3aPu8D5d1NAmQw*

Twitter: *https://twitter.com/Kim_Hayden1*

LinkedIn: *https://www.linkedin.com/in/kim-hayden-74a203181/*

Website: *https://www.resilientseries.com/kim-talks-podcast*

Resilience And Inspiration

We hope that this book has inspired you to become the resilient woman you were always meant to be. Resilience is not something we are born with; it takes hard work, dedication and a willingness to face adversity head-on in order to build it up. But if we can learn how to rise above our challenges and difficulties, then there's no limit to what we can achieve in life.

We invite you now to take your newfound resilience even further by connecting with us through our podcast and magazine series dedicated to helping women succeed in life and business. Our podcast interviews successful female entrepreneurs who share their stories of overcoming obstacles on their way towards success while also providing actionable advice for listeners so they too can start taking steps towards achieving their own goals. And our magazine features inspiring interviews from female leaders as well as articles offering practical tips on how readers can use resilience as a tool for personal growth and professional development.

So join us today for more insights into building resilience – both personally and professionally –and take charge of your life!

Resiliently, Kim Hayden

Connect with me:

Podcast: *https://podcasts.apple.com/us/podcast/kim-talks-resilience/id1563051828*

Instagram: *https://www.instagram.com/resilientseries/*

Facebook: *https://www.facebook.com/KimTalksca*

YouTube: *https://www.youtube.com/channel/UCowz4fs2_3aPu8D5d1NAmQw*

Twitter: *https://twitter.com/Kim_Hayden1*

LinkedIn: *https://www.linkedin.com/in/kim-hayden-74a203181/*

Website: *https://www.resilientseries.com*